The Beginning Filmmaker's Guide to a Successful First Film

Also by Renée Harmon

Teaching the Young Actor
The Beginning Filmmaker's Business Guide
Financing the Motion Picture
The Beginning Filmmaker's Guide to Directing
How to Audition for Movies and TV

The Beginning Filmmaker's Guide to a Successful First Film

**Renée Harmon, Ph.D.,
and Jim Lawrence, Ph.D.**

Walker and Company
New York

First published in the United States of America in 1997 by Walker Publishing Company, Inc.

Published simultaneously in Canada by Thomas Allen & Son Canada, Limited, Markham, Ontario

Library of Congress Cataloging-in-Publication Data
Harmon, Renée.
The beginning filmmaker's guide to a successful first film / Renée Harmon and Jim Lawrence.
x.   cm.
ISBN 0-8027-7521-7 (paperback)
1. Motion pictures—Production and direction—Handbooks, manuals, etc.   I. Lawrence, Jim, 1944–   .   II. Title.
PN1995.9.P7H36   1997
791.43'023—dc21   96-37637
CIP

Printed in the United States of America

2   4   6   8   10   9   7   5   3   1

Contents

· · · · · · · · ·

Introduction

In a brief interview at the conclusion of *Heart of Darkness: A Filmmaker's Apocalypse,* Academy Award–winning director Francis Ford Coppola pointed out that we are entering a time when just about everyone can become a filmmaker because the equipment is so accessible. He indicated that this might even have a somewhat radical effect on the film industry, simply because many people will be film- or video makers themselves. Some children enter elementary school having already made their own videos. Media-savvy teenagers produce so many films or videos that there is no mystery left about the process. This may lead to an audience that is more visually literate and therefore much more discriminating and sophisticated in its use of the media.

Just as children grow up with computers, they also grow up with camcorders. These technologies are merging for consumers, just as they have in the commercial industry. A number of software programs are available that allow you to import, export, and edit video and sound on your home computer, and this digitation of the media extends to the Internet and to the World Wide Web.

Both audio and video programs may be easily downloaded from all over the world and played on your own PC or Mac. Live video conferencing is also commonplace, and face-to-face video links may be established from your computer to one on the other side of the world. A genuine "global village" is definitely a technological possibility.

Computers will also be prominent in the multichannel universe. Every day more and more homes are connected to television programming via co-axial cable, fiber optics, and direct-broadcast satellite. At the same time, more suppliers are entering the mix, increasing the options for viewers. It won't be long before the familiar television receiver is transformed into a digital entertainment/information center that the consumer can program in his or her own home to suit personal needs and tastes.

What are the implications of this proliferation of programming options, with the control of these programs moved increasingly into the hands of the consumer? The presence of profanity, nudity, sexual content, and graphic violence on cable programming today is but one indication of the kinds of uncensored programming that may be available in the future. There may be channels for political extremists, religious cults, and sadomasochists, as well as for gardeners, cooks, and stamp collectors. There will be more "niche" programming directed at specific audiences with specific interests. In fact, we may very well see a limited version of what is already present on the World Wide Web on our home television or computer screens.

This new freedom may produce a lot of exciting and innovative things, but it may also produce a lot of garbage. That is the risk we have always taken in our society. We are still heirs to the Jeffersonian tradition that believes in the "emergence of truth in the free market place of ideas." In other words, put it all out there; that which has merit will last, the rest will fade away. In the final analysis, the ultimate control over the media will rest in the hands of the consumer.

No one can predict with complete accuracy what the communications industries will look like. Certainly there will be a number of new challenges. Many of these may seem overwhelming to us now, but keep this in mind: no matter how sophisticated the technology, *there will always be a need for good storytellers.* If you can develop compelling scenarios that feature identifiable characters and actually have something relevant to say about the human condition, there will continue to be opportunities for you in the industry.

You are beginning to make films at a truly exciting and promising time. *The Beginning Filmmaker's Guide to a Successful First Film* will usher you through the successful completion of your first project feature film. In Part One you'll find advice about choosing the right topic and format, writing the script, and financing and budgeting your film. Part Two helps you prepare to shoot your film, including tips on casting, the rehearsal process, and production scheduling. Part Three focuses on your first film as a career stepping-stone; there is invaluable information about entering film festivals, arranging distribution, and finding work in the film industry.

The advice given in every chapter of this book serves equally well for:

- An independent feature film
- The student films you need for class assignments
- The demo reel that showcases your work to prospective employers
- Shorts (film and video) to submit to film festivals
- Shorts required for film school acceptance

Part One

Starting Your Project

1.

Defining

Your Vision

There is no magic formula for success in film production or in the electronic media, no list of ingredients that can be stirred together for guaranteed results. Building a successful career in film and in the electronic media is often dependent upon intangible elements, some of which you may have little or no control over. Although talent, hard work, and perseverance are crucial, there are many talented, hardworking, persevering, and deserving individuals in Los Angeles, Chicago, and New York who have never gotten the break they need, and, chances are, they never will.

On the other hand, how many stories have you heard about people who were simply in the right place at the right time, or who happened to know someone who was willing to open a door for them, or who chanced to meet a potential backer who coincidentally was looking for a tax write-off? But being just plain lucky won't be enough to launch and sustain a successful career in film production or in the electronic media.

This book will provide you with guidelines and advice on how to complete a quality first project. The skills you acquire or sharpen may one day help you be technically and artistically prepared to make the most of every opportunity you have to work in the commercial film or video industry.

Take a Personal Inventory

Before you do anything else, it would be wise for you to take a realistic look at who you are, what you want, and what you are willing to do (and endure) to achieve your goals. Ask yourself some hard questions, and give yourself some honest answers.

Do You Handle Rejection Well?   There is a truism in the entertainment industry: whenever you pitch an idea, 90 percent of the time the answer will be no. *Only* 90 percent, if you're lucky. The reason is, the moment someone says yes, the project starts costing money. It's always cheaper for a producer to turn down your screenplay, to pass on your film project, to reject your idea for a video series. If you cannot adjust to this reality, you will have a very difficult time coping, both psychologically and financially.

You will need to develop a thick skin and an unshakable confidence in yourself that will see you through these inevitable down times. You will need to find something deep inside that allows you to keep going in spite of rejection. At the same time, however, you must guard against being so defensive and protective about your work that you tune out constructive criticism. You should be able to learn and grow from these experiences.

Do You Have Clear, Unbiased Knowledge of Yourself and Your Abilities?   It is very important to distinguish between realistic expectations and what is essentially idle daydreaming. Your family, friends, and relatives may gush over your amateur videos at parties, but that does not necessarily mean you are on your way to becoming the next Quentin Tarantino. You need to get feedback from a person with a professional orientation who will give you an objective critique of your work, of your abilities, and of your talent.

If you have written an original screenplay, for example, have someone read it who has no vested interest in you and who won't be concerned about hurting your feelings. Whom do you know? An industry professional? A respected high school media teacher? A university professor in a radio-TV-film department? Perhaps a friend—as long as he or she can maintain a certain degree of objectivity about your writing ability.

Similarly, screen your latest film or video project for discerning individuals or groups and carefully evaluate their critiques. Enter film, video, and screenwriting competitions and see how your work compares with others'. Ask for feedback from the judges, for specific criticism in writing.

Assessments from others are helpful, but you will have to decide for yourself whether you have the talent to realize your goals. Sometimes, however, making this judgment is not easy. It is always sad to see a young person who wants so desperately to be a filmmaker or a screenwriter, yet who clearly lacks the necessary talent or ability to succeed. But there also are several examples of people who have persevered for years, against all odds, and eventually achieved their goal.

What you will be told over and over again as you enter this highly competitive field is that you must *want* it more than anything else. This is the ultimate intangible. It has to do with a person's heart, with what's inside. This is the hardest thing of all to discern. The problem will be to align the inner dreams with the outer realities.

The bottom line is, it is okay to have your head in the clouds as long as your feet are planted firmly on the ground. Or, as Henry David Thoreau put it some years ago in an admittedly different context: "If you have built castles in the air, your work need not be lost; that is where they should be. Now put the foundations under them." (Thoreau, "Walden," *Walden and Other Writings by Henry David Thoreau,* Ed. by Joseph Wood Krutch. Bantam, 1962, p. 343)

Do You Have a Personal Point of View?   Film and video production equipment is widely accessible. Maybe you got a VHS camcorder or a Super 8 movie camera for your birthday. You are ready to make your "movie." You are anxious to point and shoot.

Now, what, if anything, do you have to say?

Point of view has to do with the way you look at life, your own unique perspective of the world in which you live. Developing a point of view—be it comic, tragic, or ironic—requires some personal experience in living, and some reflection on that experience. However, it is not necessarily dependent on age. It has more to do with your willingness right now to do some serious thinking about who you are, what you want out of life, and where you might fit in the grand scheme of things. That's right: developing a point of view requires a bit of grappling with the great existential questions of human existence and coming up with your own answers.

Traditionally, the artist, in whatever field or genre, has had a point of view, a perspective, that is communicated in and through his or her work.

Artists "foreground" our experience in such a way that it helps us to make sense of things, to see life in a different way, to connect with the great universal themes that permeate human existence. All the great books, dramas, films, and screenplays do this, and that is why they last from one generation to the next.

Give some serious thought to what you have to say. If you don't have anything to say, then why are you bothering to make a movie? If you don't have a point of view, then why are you writing a script?

You may answer that you are doing it in order to make money, or to become famous, or to win an Academy Award someday. You will find, however, that this kind of material success usually cannot be an end in and of itself. Should it come—and it may—it will come because you had something unique to say and you said it in a creative and entertaining way. Through your work you somehow managed to move people—to tears, to laughter, to thought, to action.

There is more than enough derivative work in this industry. Look inside yourself and think seriously about your own perspective on life. In the final analysis, your own point of view is the one truly original thing you will bring to whatever you do.

Are You Willing to Learn Your Craft?   There are many ways to learn media writing and production. For example, you might try some of the following:

- Take your camcorder out with friends on the weekends and make many creative and original "home movies."
- Spend all your spare time at a movie theater.
- Write your ideas down and keep working with them until you manage to turn one into a viable script.
- Work in a video store and watch every film ever put on tape.
- Read all the screenplays you can get your hands on until you teach yourself the craft.
- Watch television until your eyes glaze over.
- Hang out on a film lot or television studio every chance you get.
- Talk your way into a postproduction facility and ask all the questions you can.
- Apprentice yourself to a master craftsman and soak up everything he or she has to teach you.

- Give free labor as a production assistant or as an intern until someone gives you an opportunity to show what you can do.

All of these methods, and more, have been used by today's successful filmmakers, screenwriters, and video artists. Steven Spielberg, the Hughes brothers, and Quentin Tarantino, to name but a few, prepared themselves to work in the industry via one of the above routes.

Or you could enroll in writing and production classes in high school, or major in radio-TV-film at a college or university, or take professional courses at a trade or technical school. This is the direction taken by George Lucas, Francis Ford Coppola, Martin Scorsese, John Milius, Spike Lee, and Kathy McWhorter, among many others. However, those who went through a school or university program also gained a great deal of practical production experience at the same time. This is important to note, because classwork and school projects alone are never enough to prepare you for a career in the industry.

Ultimately it doesn't really matter which route you take, as long as you realize that filmmaking, electronic media production, and screenwriting require study, training, and practice. Raw talent is not enough. You are not born knowing what you need to know to succeed.

In this industry there is often a thin line between self-confidence and arrogance. The self-confident person is secure in his or her own abilities, but is at the same time willing (even eager!) to learn from others. Self-confidence does not preclude a sense of humility, because a truly self-confident person is not threatened by the recognition that he or she still has room to grow and improve. In fact, the filmmakers and screenwriters who have demonstrated genuine longevity in the industry, and who consistently receive the acclaim of their peers, invariably continue to hone and polish their craft throughout their entire career.

On one hand, Clint Eastwood is a perfect example of a highly successful and award-winning actor and director who has never been content to rest on his past accomplishments, and who has also been very receptive to ideas from others. Even though he always has a clear vision of what he wants to do, his films are put together in a collaborative process in which everyone seems to have an opportunity to participate. Even at the height of his success, Eastwood is secure enough to learn and grow, perfecting his craft.

On the other hand, arrogant persons adopt a posture of closure in which they appear to be unwilling or unable to learn from anyone. They think they already know everything. Since arrogance often comes from a sense of insecurity, admitting they don't know something is threatening for them. Arrogance can be a problem regardless of age or level of experience. The problem with youthful arrogance, especially in film and the electronic media, is that people end up reinventing the wheel. Because they refuse to study their craft, they assume they are the first ones to come up with a certain idea or approach, and are genuinely shocked when their work is dismissed as derivative or trite.

Are You Willing to Develop Relationships and to Network? One of the dominant realities of film and electronic media production is that you cannot and will not work in a vacuum. Even though a scriptwriter may often toil in isolation, he or she writes in order for the work to be produced, and that's eventually going to involve a number of other people. It's not like the novelist who may hide away in the Maine woods, write at his or her own pace, and then deliver the finished manuscript in three or four years. Sooner or later in film and television, the writer always has to face specific script formats, recognizable story structures, limited budgets, and inadequate shooting schedules.

If you have access to a camera, and the only thing you care about is "doing your own thing"—making what are sometimes euphemistically known as "art films" or videos—and you are not particularly concerned with actually making money or trying to support yourself in the industry, then maybe it's not important whether you develop helpful contacts. However, if you do want to pursue a career in this field, the name of the game is networking.

Simply put, networking involves cultivating individuals who may be helpful to you while you work to establish yourself as a filmmaker, screenwriter, or electronic media specialist. They will also be those people you may be in a position to assist in some way as you achieve your own level of success.

How do you meet these people? Look around! Often a network is composed of those friends from high school who helped you produce your first amateur video, or of the members of your film group in a university radio-TV-film department. It could be the team that produced that kooky radio program that aired on the campus station. Ever hear of the "USC Mafia"? That is the popular phrase used to refer to graduates of the University of Southern California School of Cinema-Television who are currently working in the film industry, persons who are in positions to assist other USC graduates as they attempt to enter the workforce.

Contacts can come from many sources. What about the people you met while doing unpaid P.A. work on that low-budget film, or when you had an internship at a television production company, the one where you made photocopies, logged videotapes, and brought coffee to the executives?

This is a small world, especially if you live and work in media centers like Los Angeles, New York, Chicago, Atlanta, Dallas, or Miami. It is absolutely crucial that you cultivate good work habits, such as dependability, promptness, and a willingness to work long hours, and that you display an enthusiastic, positive attitude, no matter what job you may be assigned. As you build a reputation for yourself, it stays with you for a long time, good or bad. Once you are typed as a whiner or a complainer or as irresponsible it is very difficult to shed the label. People talk, and prospective employers will follow up on references and call former places of employment.

Every contact is potentially important to you and you should be extremely careful that you burn no bridges as you move from one position to the next. The woman you interned for yesterday at a tiny video production facility may become a vice president of development at CBS; the low-budget exploitation director with whom you did *Blood Beast from Hell* in a New Jersey swamp suddenly could get a three-picture deal with Paramount; the nice lady you helped make her little children's videos might get a job at Disney Educational Media; the segment producer on *Entertainment Tonight* for whom you had to log endless hours of video and to run all kinds of stupid errands could have his own network show someday. You want to be remembered as a hard worker with a good attitude. If there ever was an industry where this cliché is true it is this one: what goes around, comes around!

Maintain an address book and keep it current. Make periodic calls. Touch base. Say hello. You know the word *schmooze?* There are some terrifically successful people in the entertainment business who may not be all that talented themselves, but who have turned schmoozing into an art form, and it is on that skill alone that they have built their entire careers. This may be distasteful to you. You may, in fact, believe that socializing at this level is selling out to commercialization. Perhaps you believe that, by definition, "true artistes" are essentially antisocial neurotics and you must therefore act in kind. If so, you will have a very difficult time creating and maintaining a career for yourself in either film or the electronic media.

Can You Define Your Goals?   Assuming you answered yes to the previous questions, the next thing you need to do is define both short-term and long-term goals for yourself. Where do you see yourself in six months? In one year? In three years? In five years? Do you want a job, or do you want a career? If the latter, what kind of career do you hope to create for yourself?

If you want a career in film or the electronic media, it is certainly preferable to work in that environment than it is to work in some totally unrelated field. Better a mail boy (or girl) on the Warner Brothers back lot, for example, than a server at a fast-food restaurant. For that reason, in the short term you may very well have to think in terms of doing whatever it takes to get on the inside. There is something to be said for the "I'll-do-anything" approach, if it opens the right door for you. However, you must recognize that there are literally thousands of people knocking on doors in media centers across the country saying the same thing. What makes you stand out from the teeming masses? What do you have to offer that might give you the edge?

The key is that you will eventually have to develop some asset or commodity that people in the industry want and for which they will be willing to pay. If you are a writer, that commodity will be a viable script with commercial potential—or at the least, it will be a sample script that demonstrates your ability to write such a viable commercial script. If you are a director, that commodity will be more complex and more subjective. It may include an original script to which you attach yourself as director, and there are many recent examples of just such an entreé into the industry. It will also include your ability to tell a story in visual terms, your sense of timing and pace, your ability to work with actors and production personnel, and your ability to bring in a project on time and under budget, to name a few.

In other areas, you must demonstrate your ability to deliver before anyone is going to take a financial risk to give you your big break. If you want to be a cinematographer or a videographer, you must have a demo reel that shows off your "eye." Want to be an editor? Then you must be able to demonstrate on film or video how you can effectively cut images and sounds into a compelling story. Want to be a producer? Then somehow you must be able to prove that you have what it takes to pull a project together and to deliver it on time and on budget.

What if you want to move into areas for which you have no direct preparation? For example, you are interested in digital postproduction and/ or nonlinear video editing, but you have no opportunity to learn this at your current school or university. Interestingly enough, in these days of technological development, it is possible to move into these new and rapidly developing fields simply because most production facilities expect to retrain their employees anyway. If you have a solid background in basic video production, a willingness to learn, good work habits, and a positive attitude, a company may be interested in taking you on and providing the necessary training for you as an investment.

The point is, sooner or later you will be well advised to set specific goals for yourself and to start to devise a carefully thought-out plan that will help you to obtain them. You may begin by thinking that you would be willing to do anything in the industry, but you cannot be a generalist for long. It is simply too competitive. *What do you do well, and how can you exploit that skill?*

2.

Deciding

on a

First Project

What do you want to accomplish with your film or video project? This is an important question, because it will have significant implications for what you will be able to do with your project when it is completed.

If all you care about is making videos or Super 8 movies with your friends that can be shown at parties for laughs, then perhaps this book is not for you. That is not to say that professionally oriented film and video production lacks fun and excitement. On the contrary, many people are attracted to the industry precisely because of the "adrenaline rush" they experience when working in the field. Somehow the long hours, hard work, and many interpersonal conflicts all seem worth it when the final product is projected on a big screen or broadcast to a nationwide audience. Like any craft, professional film production has certain demands and expectations that you will do well to acknowledge if you hope to use this project to achieve your long-term goals.

Slice-of-Life, Caught-in-the-Act, and Domestic Videos

"Hey, hon! Look at what the kid's doing! Quick! Get the camcorder and let's get him on *America's Funniest Home Videos!*"

With the proliferation of relatively inexpensive camcorders, just about everyone can be a videographer these days. Entire shows on the networks, on cable, and in syndication are made up of nothing but slice-of-life videos shot by nonprofessionals from all over the world.

Sometimes these videos are crudely staged, sometimes they are simply "happy accidents," but all of them tend to have at least two things in common. One is that most of them are made by amateurs with little skill or training in film and/or video production. The other is that the subject or the event takes precedence over aesthetics or technique.

If you capture a funny bit at Junior's third birthday party, it does not really matter if the shot is out of focus or if the camera shakes or if the white balance is off. Because of our emotional attachment to the content of the scene, we are willing to forgive technical flaws. We are happy just to have some kind of record of this historic occasion.

The same could be said for those caught-in-the-act videos where celebrities are recorded in embarrassing situations, or when potentially criminal activity is spontaneously taped by someone who just happens to be in the right place at the right time. It is more important that we see the bribe being passed from the gangster to the politician than it is for the camera to be firmly set on a tripod. Again, the content of the scene takes precedence over the filmmaking skills of the videographer. Because of our interest in the subject matter, we will overlook a grainy, unstable, out-of-focus image.

One thing you should be aware of is that these kinds of amateur videos rarely (if ever) lead to a career in film production or in the electronic media. They are indeed ends in and of themselves. Think, for example, of the infamous home video that depicted Rodney King being kicked and bludgeoned by Los Angeles police officers. The impact of those images was powerful and far reaching. The man who made the video may have had his "fifteen minutes of fame," but he has not parlayed that video into a career in the media.

Graduations, family or class reunions, bar mitzvahs, weddings, christenings, receptions, awards ceremonies, athletic events, and other such activities provide abundant opportunities to make videos. Even in the best of circumstances, the coverage of these events often displays the same kinds of technical and aesthetic flaws discussed above, and the subject matter is usually of real interest only to those people involved. On some occasions a videographer may be hired to do the taping and sometimes to edit the raw footage into a semipolished presentation. In fact, producing these kinds of personal or domestic videos can be a source of part-time income for student filmmakers. Rarely, however, will such a domestic video be the key to advancement into the commercial industry, no matter how creatively produced they are.

Verité Style and the Documentary

There is a style of filmmaking that bears some resemblance to the amateur slice-of-life or caught-in-the-act videos. It is called verité style and it usually refers to films or videos that attempt to capture life as it is, without imposing any kind of "artificial" structure on it. No script, no preplanning, just a desire to capture objectively on film or tape events exactly as they unfold in front of the lens.

Now, one might well argue that the moment you point a camera at something you have already imposed a kind of structure on it, and one might further argue that there really is no such thing as true objectivity when it comes to film or video, but be that as it may, the point here is to look at the implications of the production style itself. To shoot what is known as cinema verité often means that aesthetic judgments and professional production techniques will be sacrificed in order to follow the action and capture the reality of the moment. The camera may be unsteady; shots may be out of focus; exposure may be off; microphones, lighting instruments, and even members of the film crew may appear in the scenes. None of this matters if the subject is compelling enough.

If your ultimate goal is to produce these kinds of films or videos—and there are a number of highly respected and award-winning filmmakers who work in this genre—then there is certainly nothing wrong with starting on this track with your first project. If the subject draws our attention and engages us emotionally (and that's a very big "if"), it may overcome whatever aesthetic or technical problems there might be in the final product. However, if your goal is to work one day in the commercial film or television industry, such a project may not serve to advance your career in that direction. It will tell a potential employer virtually nothing about your ability to deliver a film or video production on time, on budget, and with recognizable professional quality.

A documentary may sometimes use elements of a verité style, but in most cases it involves considerable research and production planning. If there is not a complete script, there is often in its place a rather detailed outline that explores all the various issues to be addressed and lists the people, places, and things to be shot. There is a story to be told, a problem to be explored, an event to be described, a person's life to be examined. Even if a documentary uses footage from spontaneous or unpredictable events (a protest, a riot, an arrest, a battlefield skirmish), it usually tries to place that material within some kind of planned and organized structure.

If your goal is to become a maker of documentary films or videos, you might as well prepare to spend your life scrambling for money. The very nature of the documentary process works against the whole idea of profitability. Many projects extend over long periods and focus on subjects with limited appeal or interest. This is not to say that such projects are not worthy of pursuit, it is simply to point out that the production of documentaries often requires a great deal of personal and financial sacrifice.

Successful documentarians most often produce their work for video, cable, or broadcast, though there are some documentaries that are produced initially for theatrical release. In fact, every year the Academy of Motion Picture Arts and Sciences honors films in this category and occasionally a highly acclaimed documentary may actually achieve widespread theatrical distribution. However, such occurrences are rare.

A well-made documentary about a compelling subject or person may open the door to work in television news, in public broadcasting, in cable programming, in educational media, and in a number of other areas. It may also provide an opportunity to win festival awards and receive other kinds of public acclaim. It is a production technique with a long and honored history and one that has had considerable influence at a number of key junctures in our nation's history. However, without exception, a successful documentary producer needs to have a genuine passion about his or her work. It almost has to be a calling. Do you have the personal commitment for this kind of film or video production?

The Docudrama and Reality Programming

Docudrama is dramatic re-creation of actual events. What sets it apart from a fictionalized story is that it purports to be true, or at least is based on things that really happened. It may look like a documentary or it may look like a dramatic film or television program in its approach. It may use professional actors, or in some cases it may use the actual people who are re-creating their roles in these real-life events for the camera. Whatever approach the docudrama takes, its appeal lies in its claim to be based in reality.

One of the characteristics of a docudrama is that it uses the production techniques of drama to re-create the story. In other words, there is usually a higher standard required, which means that the flaws of amateur filmmaking are no longer acceptable. A dramatic re-creation is approached the same way a fictional story would be, and therefore the director must be concerned with higher levels of aesthetic quality and professionalism. No more unsteady cameras, out-of-focus shots, underexposed scenes, and shaky zooms.

There is still a great deal of what is called reality programming on television, and if this is your interest, working with both documentary and docudrama techniques might be good preparation. As of this writing, *Unsolved Mysteries* and *America's Most Wanted* continue to enjoy success in first run and in syndication, and both rely heavily on dramatic re-creations. Shows like *Cops, True Stories of the Highway Patrol,* and even some of the so-called tabloid shows often use this style in reporting their stories. In fact, a number of full-length movies made for broadcast television and cable are essentially docudramas, though considerable liberty is sometimes taken in depicting the facts of the story. The continuum may run from HBO's *And the Band Played On* and TNT's *Amelia Earhart* to the three different versions of the Amy Fisher story that aired on three different networks, each purporting to be true.

One of the best ways to learn this style of filmmaking is simply to watch those programs that use it and to study the production techniques involved. Both docudrama and reality programming will probably continue as viable formats for some time, because both appeal to our insatiable interest in true stories, whether they be salacious or inspirational. Also, reality programming has another attractive element for broadcast and cable executives: it is often much cheaper to produce than is a comparable dramatic program.

The Dramatic Short

Some years ago, the theatrical short subject (as it was once known) was a prime staple in motion picture programming. For example, a complete Saturday afternoon bill would often include previews of coming attractions, a cartoon, a newsreel, an episode of a serial (like "Superman vs. the Mole Men" or "Tarzan and the City of Gold"), a ten-minute short subject (known as a "one-reeler"), and a double feature, usually a pair of B-westerns starring Johnny Mack Brown or Lash LaRue—all for an admission price of twenty-five cents!

At times the short subjects were complete movie stories that were in reality elaborate screen tests for potential stars. This was especially true in the 1930s, when young unknown performers like Judy Garland, Mickey Rooney, and Deanna Durbin appeared in a series of musical shorts for MGM. This provided excellent training for the actors and actresses, and allowed the studio to gauge audience reactions to these newcomers before casting them in major feature roles. Many comic performers, such as the Little Rascals, Laurel and Hardy, and the Three Stooges, spent much of their careers doing one- and two-reelers.

Today, even though the Academy of Motion Picture Arts and Sciences still recognizes the best short subject each year, there is little market for theatrical shorts. Typically what happens is that a film may run for a week or two in a theater in Los Angeles or Santa Monica in order to qualify for an Academy Award nomination, but that is normally the extent of its theatrical distribution. Whatever future life the film has—even should it win an Oscar—will depend upon limited opportunities on public television or cable, dwindling nontheatrical film outlets, and the video sales and rental market.

Even so, there are many short dramatic films and videos produced every year, and a number of these are made by young filmmakers. Of course, if you're working independently and scrounging for every dime, producing a short film or video may simply be a matter of economic necessity. Even students in prestigious film programs, like those at USC, UCLA, or NYU, usually find that their senior and even graduate-level projects rarely run much longer than twenty minutes. The reasons for this are partly economic, partly academic, and partly pragmatic. Also, the fact of the matter is that you can tell a great deal about the creative potential of a filmmaker in a ten-minute production.

Some short dramatic films and videos are the works of established industry professionals. For example, a successful actor or actress interested in moving into directing may matriculate in a program for independent filmmakers, like the one developed by the American Film Institute, in order to produce a short film as a kind of demo. Normally they do this not to make money from the effort but to use the completed project to change the direction of their career.

If you decide to make a dramatic short—that is, a tightly scripted story that can be told effectively in less than thirty minutes, using skilled performers and a capable technical crew—you should approach it in light of your long-term career goals. Specifically, what do you hope this project will accomplish for you? Chances are, it is not going to make you rich. You might as well forget that right now. So be clear about why you are making it.

If you are reading this book, it is probably safe to assume that you have moved beyond the fooling-around-with-your-buddies stage of filmmaking. This is not to devalue this experience in any way. In fact, many successful filmmakers started out precisely like this. For example, Albert and Allen Hughes *(Menace II Society, Dead Presidents)* began as small boys by making all kinds of "movies" with their parents' camcorder, and the Cohens *(The Hudsucker Proxy, Miller's Crossing, Raising Arizona)* learned very early on how to improvise and experiment in order to create the effect they wanted on film, without much money, equipment, or other resources. Sooner or later, however, they began to direct their focus toward a more professional orientation that distinguished their filmmaking skills and demonstrated their ability to work at the accepted industry level. This is precisely the kind of focus you will eventually need to show in your own productions if you hope to open the door to a job or a long-term career in film production or in the electronic media.

about when it is composed of abstract animated images synchronized with nonmusical sounds generated by a synthesizer? What does a video mean when it is made up of computer-generated three-dimensional geometric patterns that constantly morph from one to another, accompanied a series of electronic beeps? Film and video artists attempt to explore the esthetic potential of the medium and are simply not interested in telling a linear story in the same way other filmmakers are.

What purpose could such an experimental film or video have for the beginning filmmaker? How might that advance you into the commercial industry? Other than simply providing an opportunity for you to "express yourself" artistically (you certainly should not expect to make much money in this area), experimenting on film or video, especially if experimentation is the result of using computer technology, might possibly open the door you in the fields of digital graphics, digital postproduction, and computer generated special effects.

Computer-generated effects are rapidly becoming basic ingredients in many film and video productions. Many of the special effects of *Terminator 2: Judgment Day, Jurassic Park, Cliffhanger,* and *Forrest Gump* were created using computer technology. In *Forrest Gump,* the amazing scenes of Tom Hanks shaking hands with Presidents Kennedy, Johnson, and Nixon, and the cinematic "amputation" of Gary Sinise's legs, were all accomplished by moving pixels around on a computer screen. And what is even more astonishing, those effects that used to take literally a roomful of very expensive equipment to do—if indeed they could be done at all—can now be created on a Silicon Graphics desktop PC, not much larger than a Mac Quadra. In fact, with a relatively inexpensive software package composed of *Avid VideoShop,* the *Trans-Jammer* transitional effects library, and *Elastic Reality,* you can create many sophisticated digital effects on your home computer, including morphing, warping, and numerous 3-D transitions—all for less than $700.

Animation

The art of film animation has been around since the earliest days of film-making, from *Gertie the Dinosaur* to *Steamboat Willie,* and from *Betty Boop* to the *Out of the Inkwell* comedies. Though there have been a number of successful, innovative, and very creative animators over the years—including Walter

Lantz, William Hanna and Joseph Barbera, and especially Chuck Jones and his merry team of Looney Tunes at Warner Brothers—it has been the Walt Disney Studios that have consistently been the recognized leader in the cutting edge of animation. Beginning in the 1930s with the *Silly Symphonies* and moving on to such timeless classics as *Snow White and the Seven Dwarfs* and *Fantasia,* to the more recent *Aladdin, The Lion King,* and *Pocahontas,* Disney artists elevated film animation to a recognized art form. At the same time, the Disney Studios have continued to experiment, most recently in backing Tim Burton's stop-action version of *The Nightmare Before Christmas* and in releasing *Toy Story,* the first fully computer-animated full-length feature film.

Like most film and video genres, animation is undergoing a transformation, and much of it has to do with the use of the computer. Of course, computer-generated animation has been around for some time. It is almost omnipresent in television commercials, short films, and videos. It is consistently used in features in many different ways, both to correct problems in principal photography and to generate spectacular special effects. Almost every film or video festival these days will have a number of entries in the animation category that were produced on a computer. The technology in *Toy Story* has been available; it was just a matter of taking the time (about four years!) and investing the money to turn it into a feature-length project.

The standard of classic animation as established by the Walt Disney Studios and others is quite high. Other films are often compared to the Disney standard and found wanting, especially those that are produced for commercial theatrical release.

There is, however, a great deal of animation that does not aspire to this kind of commercialization. Every year the national exhibition tour of the Sick and Twisted Animation Festival compiles a collection of independently produced animated films that runs the gamut from crude and disgusting to slick and dazzling. This and other such festivals all around the world give abundant evidence that there are many filmmakers working in animation, and that they are experimenting with every possible form. In fact, one of the exciting things about these noncommercial animators is their willingness to explore and innovate. Since many of them are working with very limited resources, sometimes this creativity arises out of necessity, resulting in some startling surprises.

Animation is time consuming and expensive, whether created by drawings, clay, stop action, or computer. Even one- or two-minute videos may take weeks of painstaking work to produce. A five-minute film or video that features full animation requires literally thousands of separate drawings (or clay positions, or camera setups, or computer graphics). Even limited animation takes a great deal of patience to complete a satisfactory project. A career as an independent animator is almost impossible unless you somehow work your way up through the ranks to the point where you have your own company and can work for yourself. The simple fact is, you are going to have to work *for* somebody, and you should prepare yourself for that reality.

Happily there is a lot of animation being done these days. We have certainly seen a revival of the theatrical animated film, and there is still a great deal of first-run animation on both broadcast television and cable. The Disney Studios and others have apparently made a long-term commitment to the art form, and this means that they will be on the lookout for talented young artists to enter an apprenticeship with experienced animators. However, even though there are opportunities in animation today, you should know that much of the ink and painting work is actually produced overseas, most notably in Japan and Korea. This is especially true in television animation, where budgets are much tighter.

If you are interested in producing an animated film or video for your first project, you should (as always) think about what you expect it to accomplish for you. Surely this could be a demo that can show off your work for a potential employer. Creativity, originality, and genuine talent will always catch the eye of someone in this field, but you should also study the work of different animators or studios and try to emulate a style you admire. Take careful note that the animation in *Pocahontas* is light-years away from the animation in *The Simpsons*. It is not to say one is better than the other, it is simply to point out that there are many different approaches to the art form. If you want to work for the Disney Studios one day, you might do well to think about creating something that would catch their eye.

The Music Video

Producing a music video often has great appeal to young filmmakers, who are exposed to many of them on MTV, VH-1, and on the Nashville Network. Music videos appear to be fun to make, and you can certainly do lots of creative things with them. In fact, the music video seems to give the filmmaker a license to do just about anything he or she wants. On the surface, there appear to be few rules to follow, so anything goes.

These days it is essential for rock, pop, and country performers to produce videos of their work. Indeed it is difficult to have a hit if your song is not being shown on the major cable outlets. But it is clear that the quality of music videos varies greatly from artist to artist. Some groups struggle to scrape up a few thousand dollars just to get their band on tape, usually combining grainy live concert footage with miscellaneous (and often irrelevant) shots of the musicians frolicking on the beach, gazing wistfully into space, or trying to emote meaningfully while wandering down a graffiti-scarred alley. At the other extreme, it is not unusual for major artists like Michael Jackson, Paula Abdul, or Madonna to pump $2 to $10 million or more into the production of their videos—roughly the equivalent of a "high-end" television movie or a low-budget feature—and the results clearly show this artistic and financial investment. They become mini-movies in every way, and some, like Michael Jackson's *History,* feature an extensive use of expensive and sophisticated computer-generated special effects.

If your interest lies in music videos, there is nothing wrong with producing one as your first project. You should realize, however, that making low-budget amateur music videos may encourage some bad filmmaking habits that could hurt you later on. Partly because of a lack of money, partly because of a tight shooting schedule, partly because of a misguided idea of what cinematic style actually is, many of these projects are full of sloppy camera work, mismatched edits, and a nonexistent continuity. Often there is no sense or logic to the sequence of images that are cut together. Ironically, instead of being original, many of these projects are actually derivative. The video of one group starts to look very much like the video of another, only the song is different.

Producing one music video may prepare you to produce more music videos, but it does not necessarily prepare you to work in other areas of the industry. For example, it rarely demonstrates that you can tell a linear story in an effective and compelling way, or even that you can work with actors who actually have lines to memorize and scenes to play with other actors. In fact, it often puts you in a position of having to explain away the bad acting by the band members and their groupies.

Though there are examples of filmmakers who have managed to move out of music videos into some form of mainstream filmmaking, they are not many. On the high-end productions, like those of Madonna or Michael

Jackson, for example, where millions of dollars are at stake, it is often the other way around. It is more likely that an established theatrical director like John Landis, who directed *Thriller* and others, would be brought in to oversee the project.

The Religious Film or Video

The nontheatrical market for religious films has changed radically over the past twenty years. There used to be a number of dealerships all over the country that provided a distribution outlet for 16mm films. The dealer would purchase prints from producers like Family Films or Cathedral Films, then turn around and rent these films to churches, schools, and synagogues. For example, a dealer would purchase a 16mm print of Family Films's 45-minute film *Truce in the Forest* for $425, then rent it out at $40 a showing. Obviously, the dealer needed to rent the film some eleven or twelve times to recoup his investment. At the other end, Family Films would need to sell at least 100 prints of the film to get back its $40,000 production cost. Their goal, of course, was to go far beyond this and to sell 300 or more prints of each title (which was indeed feasible). The system worked as long as there were a number of potential distribution outlets and the producer could sell multiple prints to each. Though there was never a lot of money to be made in religious filmmaking, there were still the occasional "hits" (such as *Thief in the Night*) that managed to generate considerable income in the nontheatrical rental circuit.

This has completely changed. Most of the active dealerships of the fifties, sixties, and seventies have long ago gone out of business. The small mom-and-pop religious film outlets do not exist anymore. Since it is no longer possible to make a profit by exclusively producing 16mm religious films, most of the companies that once specialized in this area have ceased to exist, turned into distributors only, been absorbed by some larger entity such as a publishing house, or now make only very low-budget videos—many of them on highly specialized subjects—for direct sale to consumers.

It is probably fair to say that the biggest change in the religious market over the past few years has been the switch from film to videocassette. Many schools and churches have their own VCRs and monitors, often in every classroom. It is much more convenient to pop in a videocassette than it is to set up a 16mm projector and show a film. The films are still out there and are still being used, but not nearly as much as they used to be. What rentals there are now are concentrated in denominational, school, or university media centers, supplemented by the few viable commercial rental outlets that still exist in various parts of the country.

If you come up with an idea for a short film that might have appeal in the religious markets—and, ironically, the subject matter does not have to be overtly religious in order for it to be widely used—your best hope is to have it distributed on video for direct sales to schools and churches. Your next-best bet is to get a distribution deal where you retain a percentage of both sales and rentals. In either case, unless you have created something very special that generates enormous demand, it will be imperative that your project end up on videocassette. There are a few feature films made for the religious market. Most of them are produced by the Billy Graham organization, and they seem to make one only every few years.

Unfortunately, there are very few opportunities to build a career in religious filmmaking, especially as an independent, and this is something you should keep in mind. Another thing you should consider is that it is very easy to become typecast when you work in this area, and there seems to be a kind of prejudice in the commercial film and television industry against producers of religious films and videos. There are some wonderfully talented writers and directors who have created award-winning projects in this field, yet who have never been able to move beyond it and achieve any significant success in features or on broadcast or cable television.

If this is truly your calling, however, you should go for it. Some films that have become classics in the field—like Rolf Forsberg's powerful short film *Parable*—last for years and may have a profound influence on the people that see them. It is, indeed, a kind of ministry, and perhaps this is reward enough in and of itself. Just realize, however, that your career choices will be limited and that you may very well need to support yourself by doing something else.

The Demo Reel

Ultimately, one reason for producing a film or video project is to create an example of what you can do, a showcase for your talent and ability. In fact, it is very common in the industry these days for artists and craftsmen from almost every area to put together a VHS cassette that they can then make available to potential employers.

A specifically designed demo reel is usually not a complete film or video program in and of itself. In fact, most rarely run longer than five or ten minutes. For example, actors often have video demos that include one or more scenes that display their range and how they appear on camera. Cinematographers may put together a series of clips on a cassette that illustrate their ability to use framing, composition, camera movement, and lighting. A second-unit director or stunt coordinator wanting to show that he or she could stage and direct action might create a short film or video that features an exciting chase of fight sequence, or that demonstrates an ability to work with stunts and special effects. Such demos are "teasers" that might prompt a potential employer to see more of your work.

What is important is that the demo reel shows off what you intend! It is meant to be distributed to someone who is in a position to hire you, finance you, recommend you, provide you with grants, or in some way advance your career in film or in the electronic media. When this person views a sample of your work, he or she should get a clear and immediate impression of what your strengths and assets are. You want to present yourself in the best possible light.

At no time should you submit a demo reel that is accompanied by an apology or an explanation. It must stand on its own merits. If you cannot in good conscience submit such a sample of your work, then you better wait until you can.

Obviously, the demo reel is a special case. It is made for a limited but, at the same time, very important audience. It is not, however, normally something that one intends for general audience distribution and therefore it is not something that has any direct commercial potential. Nevertheless, if the primary reason for producing this project is not to make money but to open the door for additional opportunities in film or electronic media, then the creation of a good demo real is certainly one viable option.

Sizzle or Fizzle?

Erotica, pornography, and obscenity are fringe areas of film and video production that usually lead to dead ends. Judging whether something is erotic is highly subjective. What one person finds stimulating and provocative, another may find to be completely offensive.

Opportunities for legitimate filmmakers in the "adult film industry" are rather limited. Most people work in relative obscurity, producing low-budget films and videos that achieve only limited distribution. Director Zalman King, with his cable anthology *The Red Shoe Diaries* and a series of feature films, is an exception, having built a rather successful career in the mainstream industry.

What is the difference between eroticism and pornography? Once again the answer is subjective. As a filmmaker, you should know that certain material may not only be pornographic but also be against the law! If you produce something that can be legally classified as obscene, you may end up paying a hefty fine and spending a long time in jail—and your career will be over before it gets started. If you think you might be dabbling in this area (and we strongly caution against it!), you would be wise to acquaint yourself with the latest Supreme Court rulings on obscenity (see Appendix A).

Violence is another area where the filmmaker needs to tread cautiously. Gratuitous or excessive depictions of violence, shown solely for its own sake, are socially objectionable and artistically weak. How you deal with violence in your own films and videos is something you will have to decide. Give some careful thought to your decision, and handle such material with a sense of responsibility, integrity, and good taste.

3.

Making the Best of

What You Have

Take a look around and determine what resources you have that will help you successfully complete a first film or video project. Once you know what you have and what you can get, you will have a pretty good idea of what you can realistically accomplish.

Before you do anything else, however, you should take a close look at the story you want to tell. What shape is it in? Do you have a well-written script prepared in the proper format? Does it say precisely what you want it to say in the most effective and efficient way possible? There will be much more about scriptwriting in chapter 4, but for now you should think of the script as the blueprint for your production. An industry adage says "If it ain't on the page, it ain't on the stage," and this should be your guiding principle as you produce your first project. In the long run, a good shootable script will save you all kinds of grief.

Once you have the story you want to tell down on paper, after you have written and rewritten until you have gotten it precisely in the shape you want it in, then (and only then) it is time to determine what it will actually take to get it made. In the industry this is called breaking down the script, and it is usually done by the unit production manager or the first assistant director. Once the script is broken down, it is possible to plan an appropriate shooting schedule and to project an accurate budget. These aspects of preproduction are discussed more fully in chapters 6 and 10, but at this point it is important for you to know that it is a necessary part of the process. Do yourself a huge favor and resist the temptation to grab a camera and start shooting before you have planned out carefully what you want to do and how you hope to accomplish it.

Now, assuming you have a good script in hand and some clear idea of what it will actually take to produce it, you should do an inventory of your liabilities (to see how you can overcome them) and your assets (to see how you exploit them).

Possible Liabilities: They Don't Have to Weigh You Down

• Inexperience is a big hurdle for the student filmmaker. Completing a well-made film or video project requires an understanding of the entire production process, from the technical to the aesthetic, and this is something that has to be learned. It also necessitates working with and depending upon others; some people have a lot of difficulty doing this. Don't be daunted by your lack of experience. Whatever you don't know, you can learn—and reading this book is a step in the right direction.

• Enthusiasm is a definite asset, but it can be a liability, too, if it is not balanced with a good strong dose of critical reasoning. It is very easy to get carried away in a rush of excitement and start making decisions from the heart instead of from the head and neglecting a lot of important details. The trick is to maintain your enthusiasm while focusing on all the hard realities involved in completing a well-made project.

• Not knowing how to accept advice and suggestions can lead to all sorts of problems. Since you will be involved in a collaborative effort, there will often be a difference of opinion concerning how things ought to be done. To whom do you listen? How do you know when to stick to your guns and when to compromise? This is the time to make informed decisions, to draw upon everything you have ever read, seen, and thought about (another reason you need to learn your craft thoroughly!), and it is the time to be guided by good old common sense. It is amazing how many young filmmakers permit sanity and sensibility to fly out the window as soon as they get their hands on a camera!

• Speaking of friends, they may become a liability if you depend on them to do jobs for which they are not prepared. Nothing is more frustrating than to be stuck with a bunch of well-meaning buddies who are doing you a favor by helping you out, but who are unskilled or incompetent. If things really get out of hand, you may be faced with a difficult decision: is it more important to produce a quality film or video or to keep your friendships intact? There will be a lot of pressure in the best of circumstances, especially when you are working with limited time and resources. Don't put your friends in this difficult position if you know in your heart they will not be able to do the work.

• Failure to have a realistic take on your own abilities and shortcomings can be a major liability. This has been touched on previously, but it won't hurt to mention it again. There is no room for posturing here. If you don't know something, find someone to ask. You don't have to feel threatened because you feel insecure about the process, which can be overwhelming at times. Even Steven Spielberg admits that he has butterflies on the first day of a shoot, and is beset by moments of self-doubt, wondering if he will be able to pull it off. It is not a sign of weakness to admit you still have something to learn. It can be disastrous, however, to pretend you know something when you don't. You have strengths; you also have weaknesses. Learn what they are and find out how to deal with them in the most positive and effective way possible.

• Trying to do too much is a liability. Young filmmakers sometimes have a great deal of difficulty in delegating authority and depending on other people. As hard as this may be, you are going to have to learn how to do it if you want to work in this industry. No matter how tempted you are to wear all the hats, remember, you have only one head. It is entirely possible that you have written a script that you plan to shoot, direct, and edit yourself. Maybe you want to star in it, too. This kind of ultimate *auteur* filmmaking is possible (if difficult), but it may place rather severe limitations on the quality of the final product. Instead of trying to do everything yourself, why not start now learning how to work in a collaborative art form?

• Lack of money, equipment, and other resources will definitely be a liability, unless you happen to be specially blessed with all the assets you need. This is something that can be overcome, however, and throughout this book you will be given some suggestions on how to deal with this situation. But you should know right now that this is one problem that will *never* go away, no matter how successful you become.

Potential Assets

• Inexperience can be an asset or a liability. There is definitely something to be said for the energy and enthusiasm that come with youth. Sometimes not knowing the established way of addressing a problem is an asset, because you attack it without any preconceived notions and may actually come up with an even more creative solution. A sudden burst of inspiration can cover up a lot of inexperience. *Sometimes.* So nurture your enthusiasm, go with your inspiration—but learn your craft as well.

• If you own equipment, like a Super 8 or a 16mm camera or a camcorder, then maybe you can work with that and supplement it with what you can borrow or rent. Maybe you have friends or acquaintances who have access to various resources that you may use for little or no compensation. Cheap is good, free is better. In *Hamlet,* Polonius advises his son "neither a borrower nor a lender be"—but then Laertes never tried to make it as an independent filmmaker. Don't be bashful; don't be afraid to ask.

Actually, some beginning filmmakers start with an inventory of their resources, and then write a project around what is available to them. Rather than creating a script that calls for a level of production they know they can never achieve, they focus on what they can do with what they have. In a way, this is what Robert Rodriguez did with *El Mariachi.* Many of the elements in the film (including the school bus sequence) are there because Rodriguez knew in advance he had access to them, and that they would cost him little or nothing. Some basic choices, such as whether to shoot on film or video, may also be determined by what is actually available to you.

Make a list. What do you own or have access to? What can you borrow? How many resources can you put together before you actually have to spend any money? Think carefully about this. You might be surprised at what you find.

• If you are a student in a high school or university film or television program you may have access to equipment and facilities owned by the institution. This access varies greatly from program to program. Some place restrictions on student access to their resources; others limit the use of equipment to those students who are actually enrolled in film and video classes, and whose projects are officially approved as part of their academic program.

Most programs have a supply of cameras, tripods, dollies, light kits, microphones, tape recorders, and other kinds of production equipment that may be available to you if you go through the proper channels. Most also have a sound stage or television studio, and some film or video editing facilities. Once again, whether these resources will be available to you for your own project will depend on the policies of the school or university, and on whether you are enrolled in the appropriate program.

• If your project happens to be part of the school or university curriculum, this is a definite asset. You will then have the added advantage of receiving advice, guidance, and evaluation from a teacher or professor. Being part of a structured program may help you avoid some of the problems that often plague beginning filmmakers who are trying to work on their own. Many radio-TV-film instructors have had (or continue to have) careers in the commercial film and video industries, and they supplement their academic classroom teaching with a great deal of practical experience. This is your chance to learn from someone who has "been there, done that."

In fact, one of the main reasons for enrolling in a film or video program is to take advantage of this kind of feedback within an educational and supportive environment. You'll find this is not so easy to come by outside a classroom situation. It only works, however, if you stop looking at your work as a series of class assignments you must complete for grades, and start looking at them as opportunities to learn your craft and to compile a film or video résumé of your work.

• It can be an asset for you if you live in a major production center where there are actors, professional technicians, sound stages, and equipment-rental houses. Independent filmmaking is all about cutting deals, and young producers can be quite creative about this. For example, if you live in or near Los Angeles there is a large reservoir of actors, many of whom will appear in student films. They do it for the experience and the exposure, and sometimes only ask for a video copy of the production in exchange for their services.

There are also many idle cameramen, soundmen, grips, set dressers, production assistants, and so on, who are available to work in student productions. They may be students themselves, they may be trying to break into the industry, or they may be between jobs or unemployed. Some will work for free, and those who expect to be paid will often negotiate their rates. Rental houses will often make deals on equipment, especially over the weekend (this actually buys you three days for the price of two), and other facilities, such as sound stages and edit suites, may be available at a significantly lower cost if you are willing to work during off hours (like midnight to five in the morning).

• Access to industry professionals is another asset in living near a production center. Get one of the annual production directories, or check the yellow pages in Los Angeles, New York, Chicago, Miami, Atlanta, or Dallas, and you will see many production companies, television stations, rental houses, labs, and other media-related businesses. If you live in one of these cities (or others with an active media production industry), and you give it some thought, you might come up with the name of a person or two in the industry whom you know or whom someone close to you knows. And the surprising thing is, many of these people will take the time to talk to you if you express a sincere interest in their work and a genuine desire to learn from someone who is more knowledgeable and experienced. This is part of the networking process.

• Your final asset is timing. Relatively inexpensive film cameras and camcorders are widely accessible, and even the consumer models are more compact and more technically sophisticated than they have ever been. Amateur videographers can actually edit their videos and include titles and a number of electronic effects in the final product. Today it is possible to put together a home production studio with a VHS camcorder, two VCRs, two small monitors, an edit controller, a character generator, and a video switcher for less than $3,000, and every single item may be purchased at a discount outlet like Circuit City or the Good Guys. Ten years ago, even five years ago, this was not possible. As a result, you may be starting out at a level of media sophistication that your predecessors did not have. You will be able to take certain technical things for granted, freeing you up to concentrate on what you want to say and how you want to say it.

4.

Writing the Script

Everything starts with the script. It doesn't matter what kind of film you want to make, the better the script the better the chance for a successful production. True, it's possible for a bad director to louse up a good script (and, if you listen to professional screenwriters, it happens all the time), but even the best director will find it almost impossible to make a good film out of a lousy script. So many disasters can be avoided in both amateur and professional filmmaking if more time and attention are paid to the writing stage. The script is your blueprint, and, like an architect's blueprint, it should be as clear and as precise as you can possibly make it. Script-writing is where you want to discover and correct problems, before you arrive on the set or on the location, where every wasted minute costs you time and money. Another industry truism is: "The small problems ignored on the page become huge problems when placed on the stage."

The Idea

Ideas are plentiful. Everybody seems to have one, from the waiter at Musso and Frank's to the bellhop at the Bonaventure, from your aunt Lucille to

When scriptwriters paint themselves into a dramatic corner and are forced to bring in something from outside to solve their problem, they have resorted to what is known as a *deus ex machina.* This term is derived from the "Golden Age" of Greek theater (Athens, ca. Fifth Century B.C.) and originally meant "god of the machine." Made popular during the time of the playwright Euripides (480–406 B.C.), it referred to the practice of suspending an actor playing one of the deities on a crane over the stage in order to resolve a hopelessly tangled plot. In essence, it means that the writer has not taken the time to build the foundation of the script. You can avoid this trap, first, by knowing the ending of your script before you start writing, and, second, with the judicious use of foreshadowing and plants.

Foreshadowing often provides subtle hints to the audience concerning potential character development and relationships. It sets up certain possibilities as the story unfolds so that the viewer has at least an unconscious awareness that something might turn out the way it does. For example, we suspect that the protagonist's alcoholism, cowardice, arrogance, or naïveté might come into play later, but we set this aside for the moment in order to follow other events. In the opening sequence of *Raiders of the Lost Ark,* Indiana Jones makes it clear that he "hates snakes!" Not much is made of this until he enters the Egyptian tomb and discovers to his horror that the "moving floor" is actually made up of thousands of poisonous snakes. When this happens in the film, the audience flashes back to that opening sequence and recalls that he hates snakes!

In this regard, the writer must walk a thin line between giving away too much and giving away too little. You don't want the audience to get there ahead of you, but by the same token you do want them to feel satisfied by the story's resolution. You want to tie all the loose ends together at the end. When the filmmaker does *not* do this, it sometimes leaves the audience a little confused or uneasy. What happened to the embryos in *Jurassic Park,* for example?

Plants often involve setting up objects, or pointing out certain skills a character has, early in the story in order to use them later in a climactic moment. In *Jaws,* there are three separate incidents in which Chief Brody has some dealing with the scuba tanks filled with compressed air. When he accidentally unties the rope securing them, Hooper warns him that the pressurized compressed air could explode. On two other occasions attention is again drawn to the tanks, reinforcing the idea that Brody has learned about their potential danger. At the climax of *Jaws,* Brody shoves one of the tanks into the shark's mouth and blows it up by shooting it with a rifle. This moment works because it was carefully set up with the effective use of a plant.

What we are talking about is structure, and, as noted screenwriter William Goldman is fond of pointing out, screenplays *are* structure. That is their very essence—having the right scene in the right place at the right time. And this is the place to determine the appropriate structure for your story, right here in the treatment. As Goldman says in his bestselling book *Adventures in the Screen Trade:*

> Writing a screenplay is in many ways similar to executing a piece of carpentry. If you take some wood and nails and glue and make a bookcase, only to find when you're done that it topples over when you try to stand it upright, you may have created something really very beautiful, but it won't work as a bookcase.
>
> The essential opening labor a screenwriter must execute is, of course, deciding what the proper structure should be for the particular screenplay you are writing. And to do that you have to know what is absolutely crucial in the telling of your story—what is its spine?
>
> Whatever it is, you must protect it to death. (Goldman, *Adventures in the Screen Trade,* Warner Books, p. 460)

Script Formats

Once you have a well-written treatment, with each scene accounted for and the dramatic structure clearly delineated, then you may move on to writing the script itself. One of the first things you will discover is that there are a number of different script formats, each designed to work with a particular kind of production. The single-camera film format is used for motion pictures, filmed television series, movies of the week, and for most short dramatic films; however, this is only one format. Multicamera situation-comedy scripts have a specific format, as do the scripts for daytime dramas, television game shows, and news interview programs. Industrial films and videos, documentaries, and interactive multimedia programs all have their own formats.

It is beyond the scope of this text to go into all these script formats, so we will demonstrate only the two that you are most likely to use on your project. The first is the two-column video script, and the second is the single-camera film script.

TWO-COLUMN VIDEO FORMAT

This is a simple format that places the video column on the left-hand side of the page and the audio column on the right.

FADE UP:	FADE UP:
Descriptions of action, scenes, and camera selections go here, lined up with the corresponding audio	MUSIC: *identifies cue and describes manner in which it is brought in and how long it stays on*
	IT *is* up full, *and* fades under, *or* fades out.
	Music may also cross fade *or* segue *to another cue.*
	NARRATOR: *these are the lines the narrator speaks.*
	SFX: *sound effects go here.*
	CHARACTER: *(the manner in which the lines are spoken). Any lines other characters have go here.*

This format is used for most in-studio video production (with the exception of situation comedies), news shows, game shows, and the like. It can easily work for a music video, news feature, or documentary.

The following is an example of a two-column script for a campus interview show.

CAMPUS RAP

Video	*Audio*
FADE UP	MUSIC FADE IN
FULL SHOT, SET IN SILHOUETTE	MUSIC UNDER
	ANNOUNCER *(VO):* Good evening and welcome to "Campus Rap," the
MAIN TITLE GRAPHIC:	show that looks at today's issues
"Campus Rap"	from the student's point of view.
	And now, here is your host of
CAMERA STARTS ZOOM-IN,	"Campus Rap," _____.
LIGHTS UP FULL	MUSIC FADE OUT
	HOST: Hello. Thanks for joining us.
	I'm _____, and tonight
	we'll be talking about _____
	_____. To help us do this
	from the student's point of view is
	my guest, _____. Hi.
	Welcome to the show.
SINGLE ON GUEST	GUEST: Thanks. I'm glad to be here.
SINGLE ON HOST	HOST: We'll get into this interesting
	topic in just 60 seconds, right after
FADE OUT	this public service announcement.
FADE UP ON	Don't go away.
PSA VIDEO ROLL-IN	SOUND: VIDEO TAPE ROLL-IN
	(TIME: 60 seconds)
VIDEO ROLL-IN OUT	
FADE UP ON HOST	HOST: We're back. First I'd like to
	ask—[HOST AND GUEST TALK
[COVERAGE: CENTER TWO-SHOT, SINGLE	FOR **4 MINUTES.** AT 3:45, GIVE
ON HOST, SINGLE ON GUEST—CUT AS	WIND-UP SIGNAL. *MUSIC FADE*
APPROPRIATE] HOST'S NAME IN LOWER	*IN UNDER*]
THIRD AND GUEST'S NAME IN LOWER	
THIRD ARE USED AS IDENTIFICATION]	HOST: Well, it looks like that's all
	time we have. I'd like to thank my
	guest, _____.

[GUEST RESPONDS]

HOST: Join us again next week for another edition of "Campus Rap."

LIGHT CHANGE TO SILHOUETTE ROLL END CREDITS	MUSIC UP FULL
FADE TO BLACK	MUSIC OUT AT END OF CREDITS

SINGLE-CAMERA FILM FORMAT

A dramatic story is probably best told using the single-camera film format, even if you are shooting on video. This format is a bit more complicated and may cause you a few headaches the first time you try it. Fortunately, if you have access to a PC or a Mac, there is screenwriting software available that will make your life much easier. *Final Draft* is a popular Macintosh program that has a new Windows version. It is also available to students at an educational discount. *Scriptware* works with DOS and Windows, *ScriptThing* works with an IBM compatible, and *Scriptor* works with both Mac and IBM. There are a number of others; some are stand-alone programs and others work with word processing programs like *Microsoft Word*. If you are seriously interested in writing for film or video, you would be well advised to invest in a scriptwriting program.

If you don't have access to a scriptwriting program, the next-best way to learn proper format is to read scripts and see what they look like on the page. Most will follow a format similar to this:

FILM FORMAT TEMPLATE

(page nos. go here) **1**

FADE IN:
(double space)
EXT. or INT. LOCATION or SUBJECT—DAY or NIGHT *(slug line or banner head)*
(double space)
Description of scenes, characters, and action are typed across the page. When <u>first</u> introduced, character names are CAPITALIZED.

References to camera movement, music, and/or sound effects are also CAPITALIZED.   *(action)*

(double space)

CHARACTER   *(character name)*

(manner in which the   *(parenthetical or*

character speaks)   *directorial cue)*

The actual line of dialog goes here.   *(dialog)*

(beat)   *(parenthetical)*

Parentheticals are set on separate line

(double space)

2ND CHARACTER

Speaks here

(double space)

If there is a break in the dialog before another character speaks, then:

(double space)

2ND CHARACTER

(continuing)

Completes his speech in this manner

(double space)

Additional descriptions of action and CAMERA MOVEMENTS are typed in this manner as needed.

TRANSITIONS GO HERE

[e.g., DISSOLVE TO:, WIPE TO:, etc. A CUT is <u>assumed</u> unless otherwise indicated.]

CHARACTER

When the speech of a character is so long
that it must go beyond its initial page, it
may be . . .

(MORE)   *(refers to dialog)*

(double space)

CONTINUED   *(refers to*

slug line)

2

CONTINUED

CHARACTER (CONT'D)

. . . continued on the top of the next page.

FADE OUT

This format is widely used in the industry. Most feature films will be written this way, as will most television movies and dramatic series. Short dramatic films should also use this format.

In Appendix B, there is an excerpt from a script for a feature film, *Heart of Silence*. Why is it important to learn the proper script format? Well, if you want to work in the industry, especially if you want to work as a screen-writer, what you write must *look like a script*! There are certain industry-wide expectations of how a script is supposed to appear on the page, and it sends the wrong message to a producer or agent if it looks like you haven't bothered to learn what these expectations are.

One other comment about writing dramatic scripts. Professional writers generally write in what is called master scene format. This means that, for the most part, they avoid "directing on paper." They concentrate on writing concise and accurate descriptions of the action, compelling characters, and believable dialog, and they leave the choice camera angles to the director. It is a given that most scenes will be shot from a number of different camera setups, but this coverage is up to the director. In fact, most directors are annoyed when they read a script in which the writer seems to be trying to do their job for them by writing in things like "ZOOM IN ON, RACK FOCUS TO, CRANE UP AND PULL OUT." Note that in the two dialog sequences in the script excerpt from *Heart of Silence*, no camera angles are indicated in the script, though it is clear that the director will use different angles to cover the scene.

Some Scriptwriting Pitfalls to Avoid

DIALOG PROBLEMS

Writing believable dialog is difficult for some people. It requires a good ear and an ability to capture the music and rhythm of the way people talk without actually recording everything they say. It is not reality; it is the suggestion of reality. Let's face it, in real life we stammer and stutter, hem and haw, repeat ourselves, contradict ourselves, and talk in circles. Transcribed literally, this would be boring! As Alfred Hitchcock once said, "Drama is real life with all the boring parts taken out." That's what good dialog should be—economical, appropriate, and, most of all, written to be spoken. Some beginning writers create speeches so convoluted or pretentious that Sir Laurence Olivier in his prime could not "speak the speech" and make sense out of it.

Some common problems are:

Use of Clichés   Upsetting apple carts, crying over spilled milk, and pulling the wool over one's eyes simply do not work in a dramatic scene (unless you want an unintentional laugh). Clichés don't have to be homilies and sayings either. Anything that becomes overused can turn into a cliché and undercut the effectiveness of the scene. Remember "groovy"? How about "dude"?

Forced or Dishonest Exposition   This is when characters tell each other things they already know, simply for the benefit of the audience. This happens in soaps all the time, because they have to catch you up to date on what happened last Tuesday when you weren't able to watch the episode. Beware of starting a speech with "As you know. . . ." If the person already knows, then why is the line being spoken at all?

Adding Unnecessary Handles   Handles are those things like "well," "look," "by the way," "so," "anyhow," and so on. When you start writing scripts you will soon discover that actors have a tendency to do this anyway, destroying the rhythm of your carefully crafted speech. You certainly don't want to give them encouragement.

Excessive Parentheticals   Parentheticals or dialog cues are those adverbs encased in parentheses under the character's name in a script. It tells the actor how to speak the line. The rule is, if the context of the scene is clear, you probably don't need one. For example, in:

JOHN:
(angrily)
You filthy son-of-a-bitch!

the (angrily) is probably redundant.

On-the-Nose Dialog   This is stating the obvious, especially in highly emotional situations. In real life, such situations usually put us at a loss for words. Whether expressing grief, venting rage, making love, or praising God, mere words don't seem to be enough. We resort to grunts and sounds on the one hand and turn to music and poetry on the other. Often when you write scenes like this you will discover that using fewer words is best.

Playing the Melodrama   On-the-nose dialog can easily turn a scene into melodrama. Melodrama is a perfectly legitimate theatrical form with a long history, and we still see it night after night in many television shows. It tends to be played at the extremes with little subtlety or nuance. If that is what you intend, fine. If, however, you are seeking some sense of realism in your work, you should try to play against the obvious when you write your scripts.

Overusing Character Names   Consider the following exchange:

SUSAN:
How 'bout meeting me for lunch, Bill?

BILL:
Sure, Susan. When?

SUSAN:
Well, how 'bout tomorrow, Bill?

BILL:
Sounds good, Susan.

Does that sound believable? When we talk with our friends or people we know, we rarely call each other by name, unless we're trying to get their attention or to emphasize something. We don't do it in real life, so don't do it in scripts.

Radio Dialog   In the days when the listening audience could not see what was happening, it was important for characters to help them out. "What are you doing with that butcher knife you have in your hand?" or "I'm walking over to look out the window now" might be acceptable lines in radio drama, but they are not in screenwriting. Even so, they creep in. "Where did you get that gun?" is a favorite. Is that what you really want to know if someone is aiming a gun at you? What do you expect him to answer? "I got it on sale at Sears for fifty-nine bucks." At that moment, who cares!

Lack of Progression   It is a principle of good speechmaking and dialog both, that when we list things we move from the least important to the most important. Consider the following:

MICHELLE: *(in apparent shock)* Secret lover! Hugh, that's insane. Why should I want a lover? I have everything: a handsome husband, an adorable baby, a beautiful home, a garden with a fish pond, a wardrobe second to none, a police dog named Prince that protects us from prowlers. . . . (Armer, *Writing the Screenplay: TV and Film,* 2nd ed. Wadsworth, p. 143)

It is clear from this speech that Michelle's husband rates far below her dog, Prince. Improper progression in a speech can generate unintentional laughs in the middle of a dramatic exchange.

Doing Funny (Peculiar) Things with Words   Actually, the writer did this to poor Michelle. How would you like to have to say, "a police dog named Prince that protects us from prowlers"? Stringing words together that all start with the same letter is called alliteration; stringing words together that all start with *p*'s and *s*'s is called unforgivable. Many things like this can be caught immediately when the script is read aloud. Keep reminding yourself that what you write is meant to be spoken.

STRUCTURAL PROBLEMS

Starting Point Too Late   There is too much wasted time in the beginning of the script before the inciting incident takes place. Remember, before this event happens the audience really has no idea of what the story is about.

Protagonist Introduced Too Late   It is taking too long for the audience to know whom to become involved with in the story. It is important that this issue be settled early on, for this character establishes the point of view or perspective from which we are to take in all that happens in the script.

Plot Points Too Early or Too Late   Though there is no hard-and-fast rule when these transitions come, it is usually helpful to try to keep the act breaks proportional. There are many exceptions, but generally in a feature film the first act ends roughly at 30 pages, the second somewhere between 80 and 90 pages, with the climax coming between pages 105 and 110. Though we have traditionally thought of a two-hour script being 120 pages, many feature scripts circulated these days are 110 or less. Transposing this to a thirty-minute film or video, the first act would come about 8 to 10 pages, the second at about 18 to 20 pages, and the climax around page 28 or 29. One reason for paying attention to this is that screenplays that are drastically out of pattern seem to have difficulty establishing consistent pace and rhythm, and this affects the effectiveness of the film.

Plot Points Not Strong Enough   By definition, a plot point must be significantly strong enough to move the story in a new direction. Some scripts, especially those that are somewhat episodic in nature, move along too much at the same level. The dramatic structure should have each episode peak at a higher level than the last.

Script Collapses in the Middle   Since the second act of the script is almost twice as long as the other two, many writers have difficulty with what is often called "the mess in the middle." The story seems to slow down until it catches its second wind near the end of act 2. One way to correct this is by setting a midpoint scene or sequence between the end of the first act and the end of the second. This works much like an act break or plot point in that it gives new energy to the story. For example, in *The Silence of the Lambs,* Hannibal Lecter's transfer to Memphis and his escape from jail happens almost in the middle of the film and raises the dramatic stakes in the story considerably.

Climax Does Not Deliver What Was Promised in the Setup   We build to the end of the story and are let down. What started out as a promising premise dissipates in the third act and becomes hackneyed and clichéd. So many contemporary films seem to fall into this trap. For whatever reason, the screenwriter has not been able to follow the storyline through to a strong (and original) conclusion.

Climax Not Organic to the Story   This raises once again the problem of the deus ex machina or the inability to resolve the story based on its own dramatic logic.

Too Many Loose Ends   Story threads are started but not resolved. Plot movements and character developments are not properly foreshadowed or planted. Unintentional red herrings appear in the script that do not pay off. The Russian playwright Chekhov once commented that if there is a shotgun hanging on the wall in act 1, someone should use it before the end of the last act. By the same token, if someone uses a shotgun in the last act, its existence should probably be established earlier in the script.

Generally, Script Is Too Dependent Upon Dialog and Not Visual Enough   Dialog is but one element that serves the film or video, and it must support the others. There are many occasions in these media when words are not only inadequate, they are unnecessary. Learn to think visually, or, as Aristotle once wrote more than 2,000 years ago, "Place the scene before your eyes."

Script Too Derivative   The story is simply a rehash of something that has been done before (and probably been done better). This comes back to one of our earlier points: you must develop your own perspective, your own point of view. Don't fall into the trap of trying to guess what might be commercial. Be original. Find your own way of saying things.

5.

How to Finance

Your Film

It is costly to produce a feature film. Even if you were able to place your film into commercial distribution, you probably would not break even, much less make a profit. We discourage you from liquidating your assets to finance your movie. Don't mortgage your home or sell your possessions. The best ways to finance your project are through loans, partnerships, and grants. The information in this chapter focuses on financing a feature film, but you can use the same options to finance shorter films.

Loans

Don't expect a commercial bank to bankroll your film. Bank loans are granted upon the "promising future performances" of a business, and that in turn is based upon previous performances. Your film, obviously, doesn't fall within the parameters of this category.

You might, however, be fortunate enough to find one or two angels who are willing to invest in your movie. If one of your relatives or friends—and we are speaking about people who are not physically involved in the production of your film—try to help you out, it is your responsibility to advise them that you won't be able to repay the loan from the film's proceeds. (Your film is unlikely to find theatrical and/or home-video distribution. And if you have been given a grant, you are prohibited from exploiting your film commercially.)

If your angels are still willing to invest in your movie and they mumble, "So what, I can use a little tax write-off," you should advise them to consult their accountant about the laws governing film tax write-offs.

For example, your dentist uncle cannot write off any monetary loss if the money he invested in your movie was taken from the income he derived from his dental practice. Only if your uncle had previously invested in a movie and made a profit from it will he be able to write off the loss incurred from his investment in your film.

You may suggest, however, that your uncle participate via an investment contract or assignment of interest of profit.

Investment Contract The investment contract offers your investor monthly interest payments for the duration of the loan, and a balloon payment at the end of an agreed-upon period. The interest you will have to pay ought to be more than your investor will earn on his or her savings and less than what you expect to pay if you were to obtain the loan from a financial institution. While you should refrain from granting your investor collateral in any of your personal assets, you might consider signing over *some* collateral rights to your movie.

Assignment of Interest of Profit   This deal grants your investor an agreed-upon percentage in your film's proceeds. It relieves you from both interest and balloon payments. But be honest about your film's chances of finding commercial distribution: let your angel know he or she may never see a penny of the investment returned.

Partnerships

Once you are ready to produce a full-length feature film to be exhibited at film festivals, a film that—if you are fortunate—might bring you a commercial distribution contract, you ought to decide upon a partnership venture involving the film's creative team:

Director
Camera director
Screenplay writer
Editor
Art director
Composer
Two to four lead actors

You, the producer, may take over any of the above positions. Most likely your team will consist of eight to ten partners, all contributing financially. Before you come to an agreement with your prospective partners, give them the following information:

· Most likely no one will see his or her money returned. No one should expect to make any money on the venture.

· You will do your best to move the film into commercial theatrical and home video distribution (domestically and overseas) but you cannot guarantee any such deals. The same holds true for screening at film festivals.

But *do* assure your prospective team:

· You will complete the film and produce the kind of professional product everyone will be proud of.

· Everyone will gain professional experience.

· Film festival screening will give all team members invaluable exposure and publicity.

Needless to say, you will only consider partners whose work you are familiar with, who have some experience via a number of student films, and who are able to work with others as a team. Stay away from egomaniacs. They may be highly creative and talented, but they can cause lots of trouble. Make certain all partners are reliable, punctual, do good work, are willing to go through hell and high water with you, and can be counted on to honor their financial commitments. Insist that every partner either deposits his or her check into the production account (not your personal account) or guarantees that certain, agreed-upon expenses will be put on his or her credit card—not an overdrawn one.

Assure your partners of your own honesty by:

- Establishing a separate production account
- Depositing your share of the partnership funds
- Having two partners countersign production checks

There is no need to form a legal limited partnership. A limited partnership can be established via legal means only. Partners invest by depositing a number of letters of credit (LC) with your bank. These LCs have to be covered by collateral, such as real-estate holdings, stocks, bonds, bank deposits. A limited partnership consists of a few active partners who run the enterprise and a number of silent partners (the permissible number varies according to state laws) who do not take part in business matters.

The partnership suited best for your purpose is the joint partnership:

- All partners are considered active partners, that is to say, all partners contribute equally in financial and creative matters. The agreement, therefore, *must* spell out each partner's area of participation.

- The agreement *must* state each partner's financial obligation and a timetable of when this obligation has to be met. In case a partner offers services either in lieu of or as part of his or her financial participation, the wholesale value of such services, not the resale value, will have to be applied.

Even a joint partnership may be fraught with pitfalls:

- Legally each active partner is authorized to "perform any services necessary to do business." This permits individual partners to incur debts "necessary to run the business." Even more unfortunate, each and every member of the joint partnership can be held liable for these debts. We strongly suggest you add a clause demanding the full agreement of all partners before any debts can be incurred.

You also may want to add an arbitration clause. Such a clause states:

· "Any claim arising out of this contract, or any breech thereof, shall be settled by arbitration according to the rules of the American Arbitration Association." (Litwark, *Dealmaking in the Film and Television Industry,* Silman-James Press, p. 118)

While you don't need an attorney to form an informal agreement, it is always beneficial to have one look over the agreement.

No discussion about financing is complete without giving some thought to the financial obligations you have to your crew members and day players who don't have partnership protection. The following are three remuneration options.

No Salaries Will Be Paid   If the majority of your crew are beginners and/ or film students who need credit or experience, they'll gladly work without pay. The same holds true for your actors. Even seasoned nonunion actors are willing to work without salary to have a showcase for their talents. If, however, you have signed a low-budget Screen Actors Guild (SAG) contract, you have to pay your actors a designated amount. The rest of their scale salary will have to be deferred upon whatever profit your film makes. Scale refers to a SAG actor's minimum daily wage, which was $400 at the time of this writing.

Deferred Salaries   Fully deferred pay (often as low as $50) is acceptable only if your actors are nonunion. Since deferred salaries will be paid from the film's profit, it is your responsibility to let actors and crew know there might be no profit.

Assignment of Interest of Profit   You assign a certain percentage of profit to each actor and crew member. Such a salary assignment looks terrific but is not worth the paper it is written on, if based upon a producer's 100 percent net profit deal. A 100 percent net profit deal is precisely 100 percent of nothing—zilch. (Only if you were smart enough to have signed an adjusted gross profit deal, to be discussed in the Distribution segment, do you stand a chance of seeing a little money come your way.)

Whatever your financial arrangements may be, it looks more professional to have cast and crew sign an agreement. Contrary to partnership and investors' agreements, you do not need an attorney to draw up this document. Regardless of whether you have decided upon deferred payment or assignment of interest, have the agreement include the following:

- Production company's (or producer's) name, address, and telephone number
- Film title
- Participant's name, address, telephone number, Social Security number, and services to be rendered
- Length of anticipated shooting schedule
- Compensation: _____ (producer's name), producer of the motion picture tentatively titled _____ (title), agrees to pay upon completion of _____ (participant's name) services the amount of _____ (daily, weekly, or lump sum). _____ (participant's name) agrees to have salary (either deferred payment or assignment of interest) deferred until first monies have been disbursed to _____ (list all accounts such as labs, investment interest, etc).
- Typed producer's name, signature, and date
- Typed participant's name, signature, and date

Grants

Most endowing organizations will fund nonprofit organizations only. You may either apply through the conduit of an organization that administers grants—and pay an administration fee after your grant has been approved—or set up a nonprofit organization and apply directly (in this case the corporation, not you, functions as the active partner in a joint partnership). But a word of warning: once you have been endowed with a grant, you are prohibited from exploiting your film commercially. While your film will be screened at film festivals, it can be shown neither theatrically nor on cable or home video. But now for the good news: receiving a grant from one organization does not prevent you from accepting additional grants from others.

Most likely you will have to contact a number of endowers before you find one interested in your project. After all, requirements do change as do the preference and taste of the committee in charge at the time of your request. It is, however, safe to consider these basic demands:

• Your film must be a low-budget project. At the time of this writing this amount ranges from $500,000 to $2 million. This, of course, does not mean your budget has to hit the half-million mark. (Don't be discouraged by these seemingly insurmountable amounts. In the next segment we will discuss a budget that has been tailored to your needs.)

• The story must take place in the United States.

• Your film must be based on a topic of either social or philosophical value. The film must have artistic merit.

The Foundation Center offers information about a great number of endowing organizations. It maintains national offices in New York City and Washington, D.C., and regional offices in about every state. You may contact them at

> The Foundation Center
> 79 Fifth Avenue
> New York, NY 10003-3076
> (212) 620-4230

Additionally, you may check your local library for these publications: *Foundation Directory* and *Foundation Fundamentals: A Guide for Grant Seekers.* More information about The Foundation Center can be found in Appendix D.

Once you have decided upon a number of organizations you wish to contact, it is time to get your prospectus ready. You'll have to submit the following documents:

• Cover page: applicant's name, address, Social Security number, and telephone number.

· Film title. Project description: a motion picture.

· Explain your project's social and/or philosophical significance: why it is a worthwhile undertaking and how it differs from other films in its field. Make it clear that your film constitutes a valuable contribution to the area you have selected to explore.

· Story synopsis (two or three pages).

· Budget: no estimates, use hard figures.

· Funds already committed to your project (if applicable). Your project will have a better chance to receive a grant if some funding is already in place.

· Résumés of key personnel to be involved in your project. Stress everyone's film expertise, experience, and credentials.

· A known and reputable film festival's letter of interest in your project. While such a letter is not one of the necessary documents to be submitted, it may prove to be extremely helpful to convince a grant-approving committee about your project's significance. Please observe that *interest* does not commit the film festival to exhibit your movie, while the term *intent* does. If you request such a letter, always ask for a letter of interest.

If possible, try to talk to someone who recently has won a grant. Try to get some information as to the style of his or her application. Some boards prefer academic presentations, whereas others like the more relaxed approach.

Legal Traps

Some legal traps may threaten your project. As you work on your film, worry about budgeting, fret over casting, and struggle with the all-important time schedules, it is easy to overlook hidden legal traps.

MUSIC RIGHTS

Your film most likely will feature music. If you had an original score composed, you won't have to worry about music rights. But if you intend to use any existing music, you better watch out.

Music, as with written matter, is protected by copyright law. The fact that the composers retain the musical copyright, while the lyricist retains the copyright of the lyrics, does not simplify matters. Or, possibly you have decided to play it safe by choosing a Handel cantata for background music. Since Handel composed during the eighteenth century, his compositions most certainly are in the public domain so you won't have to worry about copyright. Wrong. Handel's compositions are in the public domain, but if you wish to use recorded music, and the cantata of your choice has been recorded on either disc, tape, or record, you are prohibited from using the particular recording unless you have obtained permission from the recording label. You need permission for these rights:

· The right to alter a musical score under copyright.

· The right to record a copyrighted musical score, also called synchronization rights.

Fortunately, if the copyright on any composition has expired and has not been renewed, you are free to use this composition without paying a licensing fee. To make certain the copyright has expired, contact:

> U.S. Copyright Office
> Library of Congress
> Washington, DC 20559

The Copyright Office is not authorized to grant any rights, even if the copyright has expired. Only the publisher (printed music) or recording studio (recorded music) has the authority to grant these rights.

COPYRIGHT

While ideas, titles, and themes cannot be copyrighted, articles and books about living or deceased people or actual events can. If you expect to base your film on a newspaper or magazine article about an actual event, you have to obtain permission not only from the publication in which the article appeared but also from all people mentioned in the story who will appear in your screenplay.

At times, the question arises about a copyrighted screenplay's ownership. If the writer has sold his or her screenplay to a producer and/or production company, the producer or production company owns the screenplay. This is the reason that once a bank grants a production loan, it immediately takes over the ownership of the script, and as such, exerts ownership of the film in production.

If you, the producer, have optioned a script from a screenwriter, you own it for the duration of the option.

DEFAMATION OF CHARACTER

We'll have to distinguish between two kinds of defamation of character.

• Libel: defamation by written or printed word (your screenplay).

• Slander: defamation by spoken word. Here are two definitions: if a film features the experiences of a living or deceased person, and characters on screen defame this person. Or, if during a taped interview, someone connected to the production speaks ill about the person depicted in the film.

INVASION OF PRIVACY

There is a vast field open to many interpretations and misinterpretations. For instance, if you take an unauthorized picture of someone, if you dig into someone's private life, if you reveal relationships and interactions, all of these could give rise to lawsuits. Be especially wary if you shoot a documentary or docudrama. You can protect yourself from any libel suit by:

• Obtaining releases from all persons depicted in your film
• Using fictional names only
• Changing circumstances and locations so as to make these
  unrecognizable

A libel suit will not only keep your film from being exhibited but also will cost you a fortune in legal fees, and positively make your life miserable. Therefore, to protect yourself:

• Check and double-check the veracity of all facts.

• Buy an errors-and-omission insurance policy. If you want to exploit your film commercially, you need such a policy anyway.

These safeguards also apply if your film is based upon a biography or autobiography. If you wish to portray the experiences of a living person, you must have his or her permission to do so. Most likely this person will demand final approval of not only your script but of the film as well. You face a tricky situation at best. If any of the characters in your film are based upon deceased persons, according to probate laws the estate's executor, after having consulted the heirs, has the right to grant permission. If one of the descendants declines permission, however, the executor has no right to overrule the dissenting heir. Fortunately this does not hold true if you plan to shoot a film about a historical figure such as Henry III or Attila the Hun, but if you intend to trace the crimes of, say, Jesse James, you better get your permission slips ready.

6.

Your Film Budget

Before we proceed to discuss a budget that has been tailored to your needs, turn to Appendix F for a typical budget of an average low-budget film, one that won't see extensive theatrical distribution but will finds its niche in home video and on cable.

After you've seen the breakdown for a $1 million budget, you won't be quite so stunned by our mock budget that fills your specific needs. Since costs and fees change from place to place, the given amounts should be used as guidelines only. Your personal budget takes into account that all key personnel are partners who are ready to pool money, creative talents, and services.

Now is a good time to clarify a couple of terms. "Above-the-line" expenditures refers to:

- Story and rights
- Producer's unit
- Direction
- Cast (including agents' fees and actors' fringe benefits)

The term "below the line" refers to the rest of the budget. Both costs combined are considered a film's negative cost.

Story and Rights

Screenplay	Partnership participation
Idea for screenplay	$0
Photocopy 20 copies	$60

Production Unit

Producer	Partnership participation
Associate producer	Intern
Legal fees (drafting of contracts)	$200

Direction

Director	Partnership participation
Assistant director (AD)	Intern

Cast

Star 1	Partnership participation
Star 2	Partnership participation
Costar 1	Partnership participation
Costar 2	Partnership participation

CAST

Cast	No Payment

As far as your cast budget is concerned it is taken for granted that your stars and costars are active partners. It is implausible that you could afford the fee for hiring a member of SAG. If you did cast a SAG member, your production company would have to become signatory to the guild. Once you are signatory, your entire cast must be members of the Screen Actors Guild and you are prohibited from casting any nonunion actors.

Don't ever hesitate to cast nonunion actors. A majority of them are just as fine actors as their SAG counterparts. (Some union members, in fact, have no acting training at all. Anyone [primarily models] can join this union by strength of having been cast for a SAG signatory commercial.) There is no payment scale for nonunion actors. You may have to pay between $50 and

$200 a day for day players, though for our budgeting purposes, let's assume your actors will work for free.

PRODUCTION STAFF

Production manager	Intern (graduate student)
Production accountant	(part of the producer's job)
Script supervisor	Intern
Production assistant	Intern

A skilled script supervisor is very important, so look for a person who has studied script supervision. Among other things, the script supervisor is responsible for continuity. For example, if an actress wears a shawl upon leaving a building, she cannot be without a shawl as she walks down the street, though this shot may be filmed a week later. A good script supervisor can avert potential disasters during the editing process.

SET DESIGN AND CONSTRUCTION

Art director	Active partner
Assistant	Intern
Purchases	$500
Rentals	$200
Set construction	No payment

Rather than build sets, select actual locations. Try to get all these locations for free, and stay away from locations that require city permits. Once you apply for a city permit you need insurance, and depending on the location, you may be required to pay for a water truck and a (retired) firefighter. If at all possible, combine exciting stock shots with actual locations. On the film *Jungle Trap,* art director Bill Luce combined rain forest stock shots with a *dressed* backyard (used for medium shots) that even had a live boa constrictor. Rear projections can provide another means to save on location costs. In the film *Red Satchel,* which took place in Europe, actors moved in front of rear projections, creating the illusion they were strolling down a picturesque European street.

Don't ever forget to have the owner of the location sign a release:

I hereby grant _____ (producer and/or production company's name) the right to use and photograph the premises located at _____ on _____ for the duration of _____ and bring personnel and equipment onto said premises.

I _____ (name of owner) agree to hold _____ (name of producer and/or production company) free from claim for damage and/or injury arising during occupation of above premises. Producer (name of producer and/or production company) agrees to leave above location in as good condition as when received.

Signature (owner)   Signature (producer)

SET OPERATION

Key grip	Intern
Second grip	Intern
Slate	Intern

Recruit interns by sending out notices to film departments at colleges and universities. Students need the invaluable hands-on experience, which cannot be learned in a classroom. They'll also be happy to see their names listed on the "crawls." As you consider your operational personnel, be careful to hire neither too large nor too small a crew. Having too many people standing around or too few helpers struggling to get the work done slows your production down. Make certain the key grip has worked on a number of student films.

SPECIAL EFFECTS

At the time of this writing, special effects are in big demand. However, in order to grip today's audience, special effects have to be spectacular and therefore are very expensive. Even the majority of digital special effects—for the time being—are still way out of your reach. Granted, many young film-makers experiment successfully with digitized video, Hi-8 cameras, and nine-gigabyte hard drives. Yet these exciting innovations are still in the beginning stage. Our advice, therefore, is do not plan on special effects for your first project.

SET DRESSING

Petty Cash $250

Use your own possessions or borrow the items you need to dress up the set. But don't ever use sentimental treasures or other highly valued items. Things are too easily lost or broken. And you most certainly don't wish to lose a friend because you broke her aunt Mary's treasured Victorian teapot that was brought all the way from Ireland in 1895. You should use petty cash for all small, unexpected expenses, such as telephone calls away from the office, parking fees, nails or tape, and possibly such items as cat or dog food.

WARDROBE

Unless you shoot a period or fantasy picture, have actors supply their own wardrobe.

MAKEUP

Key Makeup artist   Intern
Helper   Intern
Purchases $200

Hire a recently graduated makeup artist who will appreciate having some professional experience. Have your makeup artist bring his or her own assis-tants. Some days one assistant might be sufficient, but the makeup artist may need two helpers on busier days. Although makeup artists will bring their own sponges and brushes, do not expect them to purchase makeup supplies.

LIGHTS

Gaffer	Intern
Best boy	Intern
Assistant	Intern
Lighting package	
Rentals	$300
Purchases	$200

Your lighting package is an important part of your entire production. The equipment you rent (or borrow) should be in top condition and you must have plenty of supplies (gels, bulbs, and so on) on hand. In addition to designing the light plot, the cinematographer (active partner) should direct the gaffer. The cinematographer should rent the equipment because he or she will be offered the less expensive "camera man's package."

Do not be tempted to use *fast film* in lieu of a precisely thought-out light plot. True, you will save on setup time. But fast film will taint your film with a slightly amateurish look. Instead, rent the basic "Hollywood light kit":

Lowel TOTA kit, plus	$400
Baby spots (1-K lights)	
Midget spots	

Remember, a professional light plot is mandatory if you hope to exploit your film commercially. Do not shortchange your cinematographer by expecting him or her to work with insufficient equipment. After all, the cinematographer joined your team for an opportunity to showcase a creative and exciting use of lights. Don't disappoint your partner.

Equipment rental is expensive. If you are a graduate student and are fortunate enough to have your first project declared part of your M.A. requirements, you might be given access to the film department's basic grip and lighting equipment. Still, our advice is, do rent the TOTA kit. If your cinematographer rents the package for a weekend shoot, you will pick up your equipment Friday at 5:00 P.M. (you might be able to squeeze in a few hours of night shooting) and return the equipment before 8:00 A.M. on Monday. Such a weekend package will save you lots of money, because you are only charged for Saturday.

The following is a list of the essential grip and lighting equipment.

Black backdrop curtain
Neutral backdrop curtain
Stands
Clamps
Reflectors
Prong adapters
Plug-in electrical outlet
Power cables
Apple boxes
Sandbags

There are some essentials you'll have to buy:

Gels
Diffusions
Silk (to cover lights)
Lightbulbs
Total $300

PRODUCTION SOUND

Soundperson, including: $2,600
   Boom operator
   Equipment rental
Purchases (tape) $300

Do not entrust production sound to an intern. Hire a professional who will supply his or her own equipment, consisting of:

NAGRA (no other will do)
Microphones
Boom

Get ready to spend between $200 and $300 a day for the soundperson and equipment. If you are lucky, the soundperson might give you a discount for a five-weekend shoot. If he or she wants to bring his or her own boom person, have the assistant included in the daily fee. Unfortunately, that's not all. You'll have to pay for all sound recording tapes:

Thirty rolls sound recording tapes
Twelve rolls MAG track (needed to transfer sound from
    the recording tapes used on location)

Don't try to save money on your film's sound. If you do, you will be sorry later on. Regardless of the quality of your script, your actors, your film's light plot, or your camerawork and direction, faulty sound will ruin everything you have worked for. Have your prospective soundperson do a dry run before you hire him or her. Make a recording and check the tape for static, hissing sounds, and muffled dialog. These indicate you are dealing with faulty equipment. Insist on the best sound equipment for your first project.

On an exterior location, you'll pick up some interference from street or airplane sounds. That's unavoidable. Some microphones are sensitive enough to record sounds inaudible to the human ear. If this happens, all you can do is rerecord. At times reshooting is too costly and time consuming, and if the dialog is scant enough, you may have to dub it in later on. But watch out: extensive dubbing makes dialog uneven.

If lengthy dialog is marred by continuous sound interference, do only your establishing shots on location (people walking to and from), take stills for your two-shots and reversals, and shoot the required dialog on an insert stage later on. But watch out for any light difference between the location and insert stage shots. Some of these differences will be taken care of later during your postproduction's timing procedure, whereas the more difficult lighting adjustments are your cinematographer's responsibility.

This brings us to the practice of shooting the entire film MOS (without sound) and dubbing the dialog in later on. Don't. If you do, your film will look like a foreign film that has been poorly dubbed.

Always have your soundperson record some ambience or environmental sounds, such as traffic noise, surf pounding on rocks, birds chirping, or a dog barking. You'll be able to create your own sound effects inexpensively and efficiently.

CAMERA

Director of photography	Active partner
Loader	Intern
Focus assistant	Intern
Still photographer	Intern (here a friend or relative might come in handy)
Camera package	
Purchases	$150

The expenses are rising—rapidly, we admit. If your school's camera package is available to you, count yourself fortunate. If not, our previous advice about the lighting package goes for the camera package as well. Have your cinematographer contract for the camera package. Generally such a package consists of:

Camera
Lenses
Lens mounts
Viewfinder
Magazines
Camera case
Crystal sync motor
Batteries
Battery pack
Tripod
Light meter
Changing bag
Filters
Clap board
Compressed air for cleaning camera
Matte box

Wheelchair (for the all-important dolly shots; buy one at
a swap meet)

The choice of camera depends upon your cinematographer (or upon the
camera your school has available). For reasons we will discuss as we deal
with raw stock, you ought to shoot 35mm only and therefore you'll need a
35mm camera. If you have to rent your camera and lenses, we suggest these:

- Mitchell 35mm, comes with various accessories
- Mitchell MARK II S35R Hardfront, adapts excellently for high speeds,
  and comes with various accessories
- Airflex 35 BL: self-blimped; camera noise does not interfere with sync
  sound; lightweight, can be handheld. Expensive but the very best
  for shooting sync sound. It comes with various accessories. Most
  effective to shoot extensive dialog scenes, or scenes requiring a
  handheld camera.

Whether your film school will supply you with a camera, or whether
you have to rent one, always check to be sure the lenses have been calibrated
lately and the camera runs smoothly.

And don't hesitate to pay the equipment insurance the rental company
requires. Paying for camera repairs may make your entire budget go down
the drain. A few dollars also have to be paid for purchases such as:

Gaffer's tape
Chalk and marking pens $50

TRANSPORTATION

Truck rental

Everyone provides their own transportation. If one of your active partners has access to the truck needed to transport equipment, lucky you, you
won't have to pay for a truck.

LOCATION EXPENSES

Preproduction location search
Catered meals $1,400

During the sometimes frustrating but mostly enjoyable location search, everyone pays for their own meals and gasoline.

But don't skimp on meals, especially if you have unpaid interns and actors working on your film. Plenty of appetizing and nourishing food is mandatory on a shoot. Do not ask your cast and crew to brown-bag, and do not have your aunt or sister bring sandwiches and hot coffee on the set. Hire a catering company. The money you invest is well spent. Get in contact with a company that specializes in catering for low-budget films. If you allow $7 per person and count on about twenty people daily, your bill will come to about $1,400. And make certain to have plenty of ice water available during the day.

OPTICALS

Titles $1,000
Optical sound track $2,500

Opticals such as fade-ins, fade-outs, and wipes are seldom used; a straight edit from one scene to the next is more up-to-date. For your titles and crawl, you will do best to have these first done on Beta tape and then transferred to 35mm. The cost for both will come to about $1,000.

You need, however, to take your sound tape to an optical lab to have an optical track made. The optical track shows the photographic image of your film's sound along its edge. Be aware that you need either a negative or a positive track. Both color negative stock and color reversal stock require negative optical tracks. Black-and-white negative stock requires a negative optical track, whereas black-and-white reversal stock requires a positive optical track.

EDITING

Supervising editor	Active partner
Assistant editor	Apprentice
Coding	$1,200
Projection (dailies)	
Equipment rental	
Purchases (editing and sound tape, about	
twelve rolls each)	$500

During the editing process your film moves through these stages:

• *Dailies:* developing and one light work print of previous day shoot's raw stock. After you receive your dailies have the assistant editor splice them together. Your original negative will remain in the lab's vault for safeguarding. Don't ever pay to view the dailies. Your lab ought to supply this service for free.

• *Rough Cut:* scenes are strung together in appropriate order.

• *First Assembly:* the film's weak points need to be corrected.

• *Three-quarter Cut:* the film's sound editing has been completed.

• *Final Cut:* some minor editing changes are still possible. Picture and sound track run in interlock, that is, picture and sound are projected from different sources.

• *Negative Cut:* the cut is based upon your original footage.

Some more words of advice:
Hire only a skilled assistant editor, perhaps a film school graduate who has concentrated on the editing process.
It is imperative that you have your mag/sound track and workprint coded, or in other words "edge numbered." It is nice to have the lab do this job, but if you want to save money, you can do the coding yourself. Simply attach small paper tabs to each foot of workprint and sound track. This should be done as soon as you have viewed your dailies.

Hopefully, you do have access to your school's editing facilities. If not, you have to face another major expense. You can rent either editing space and equipment for a daily or weekly fee, or editing equipment and do your editing at home. This is the equipment you need:

Workbench (you can build one yourself)
Splicer
Synchronizer (moviescope, rewinds, and sound reader)

For the purpose of our budget, assume that you will be given access to your school's facilities. Still, there are purchases to be made:

Black leader tape
Mag track
Total $300

You may save a few dollars by having your film transferred to ³/₄-inch tape and have the editing done on tape. The hourly editing rate is $35. In case you decide to preedit on tape, have an inexpensive ¹/₂-inch tape cut from the ³/₄-inch tape and make some basic editing decisions as you view the tape at home. But beware, the numbers given on your VCR do not quite correlate with the numbers on the tape-editing machine. Allow a little leeway.

MUSIC

Composer   Active partner
Musicians (if needed)   Interns

Unless the composer is among your active partners, do not bother to compose or lease your musical score. Instead, rent prerecorded music from your sound lab.

POSTPRODUCTION (SOUND)

Sound transfer
Magnetic film

> Foley
> Dolby stereo mix
> Dialog recording
> Sound FX
> Total $18,000

It's obvious that we are speaking about serious money, but do not attempt to take any shortcuts. Here are a few words of warning:

- Make certain that, for foreign sales, the dialog track can be separated from your completed film.
- If possible, have your sound effects on one track only.

RAW STOCK AND LABORATORY

35mm raw stock (ends)	$4,000
Developing and one light workprint	4,200
Negative cutting	2,500
Answer print	8,000
Two release prints	3,000
Total	21,700

Ninety minutes is just about the average length for your first project feature film. Shooting a two-to-one ratio requires about 20,000 feet of raw stock. The average price of raw stock ends is about twenty-one cents per foot. Developing and printing (one light workprint) will run about twenty-one cents per foot. Prices vary from place to place. Do not accept the first quote; try to make a deal.

While it is true that most film festivals accept 16mm and even 8mm films, in this chapter we are speaking about your first project that, if being screened at the most important festivals, will at least have a fighting chance to reach commercial distribution. For commercial distribution, a 35mm answer print is mandatory. You could save some money if you shot 16mm, but the transfer from a 16mm answer print to a 35mm answer print is expensive. In addition, because of the format differences between 16mm and 35mm, you must frame carefully so as not to have action occur too closely on either the top or bottom of the 16mm frame.

Use 35mm tested short ends. Do not buy your raw stock from a filmmaker directly; if you do, you might be getting old film. Purchase your raw stock from a reputable firm. Forget about shooting a one-to-one ratio. Forget about the friend who told you that so-and-so shot his or her prizewinning movie one to one. It cannot be done. You are not filming a stage play, you are doing a movie, and that means you have pans, dolly shots, and two-shots, and reversals, and close-ups. Shoot, if possible, 3 to one (admittedly a meager ratio), or at the very least shoot two to one. It can be done, if you have every camera move and setup mapped out precisely and you leave nothing to chance; if your actors are professionals; if sound interferences are at the minimum; and if luck is on your side.

As to how to stay within the tight boundaries of raw stock and budget, we suggest that you edit in the camera. This practice does not mean you will forgo a major editing process, and shoot action for action as outlined in the script. On the contrary, to edit in the camera means that you have decided upon and written down each and every camera move before you started shooting. It indicates that you will avoid those dangerous spurts of creativity that make you forget your planned setups in favor of some extemporaneous camera moves. Frequently such unplanned moves cause havoc during the editing process. Your "inspirational" camerawork—especially if you forgot to observe the gray line—might not cut in with the rest of the scene. We know that you the director and/or cinematographer are intimately familiar with the gray line, but for the sake of your active partner, who may be an actor or screenwriter, let us illuminate one example: according to your screenplay, *Joe enters his home.* Simple. Nothing to it. Only, the exterior of the building Joe enters and its interior are to be filmed on two different locations. Worse. Both setups are shot two weeks apart. And this means close attention to gray line (another reason why you need an experienced script supervisor).

EXTERIOR JOE'S HOME. DAY.

    Joe opens the door and enters his home. (Camera has been set up to the actor's right.)

INTERIOR JOE'S HOME. HALLWAY. DAY.

    Joe closes the door. (Again camera must be set up to the actor's right.)

Since we got sidetracked to camera setups, let's discuss one of the main concerns when directing a film: the transition from one shot to the next. As far as editing is concerned, it is beneficial to end one take and begin the next take of an editing sequence with a physical move, such as:

Reversal

End of take: actor A lifts a cup
Beginning of take: actor B rises

Exterior to interior

Exterior: car driving
Interior: actor raises his gun

Story transition

Exterior: ball thrown up in the air, pan with ball
Exterior: spaceship zooming along

Moving shot to static shot

Pan shot: angrily actor A walks to window
Cut to: actor B sitting at desk takes off his eyeglasses

Always anticipate editing problems. Therefore, use the last few feet on your roll for reaction and ambience shots. Often such shots have saved a scene when things just don't cut together.

Workprint   Some filmmakers bypass the workprint. They edit the original negative, their later answer print. Considering the many phases of the editing process, this practice is nothing but an amateurish attempt at filmmaking. Remember, the original negative cannot be replaced. Scratches and smudges cannot be corrected. The film you have worked on so diligently may be ruined for good. If, however, you are determined to travel the road of combined workprint–answer print, make certain you protect your property by having it glazed.

Negative Cut   Entrust your all-important negative to a skilled negative editor only. Your negative cannot be replaced. While the editor works on it, it must be stored in a vault (not your kitchen cabinet). If you employ your lab's negative cutter, your lab will "time" your picture for free. Timing means that color qualities will be adjusted via computer.

Answer Print   Immediately after delivery, check your answer print carefully. While it is difficult to blame the lab for scratches on the negative, it is the lab's responsibility to take care of these printing mistakes:

 • Faulty timing (color adjustments)

 • Faulty balance (the entire film has been printed too dark or too light)

 • Picture and sound out of sync. (Check your workprint and mixed sound track thoroughly to determine whether this mistake is your or the lab's fault.)

 • Faulty frameline registration (a line appears on the bottom of each frame)

Release Prints   You need release prints because you shouldn't send out your precious answer print. Keep the answer print, along with the negative, stored in your lab's vault. You need at least two release prints for film festival screenings. Since release prints are expensive, do not have any cut until you have a firm commitment from a film festival. Instead, submit ½-inch video copies of your film.

PUBLICITY

If you wish to have your film screened at film festivals, you need video copies of your film and a press kit.

Have your answer print transferred to ¾-inch video. From this, your master tape, you will cut about ten ½-inch tapes.

There is no need to get your press kit printed. Your computer will do the job just as well. The kit should include:

 • Title page with the film's title and the production company's name, address, and telephone number

· Synopsis, not more than fifty words

· List of producer, director, leading actors, screenwriter, composer, art director, editor. Give credits, if applicable.

· Black-and-white stills

INSURANCE

It would be helpful if you could obtain liability insurance in addition to equipment insurance. Your project, unfortunately, is too small to interest any company specializing in motion picture insurance. Call your insurance broker and ask about short-term insurance. Make certain that everyone on your team, including actors and crew, has car insurance. Prohibit any person who is not covered from operating a vehicle. Unfortunately, if someone connected to your project is involved in an accident occurring either on the way to work or back, the active partnership could be held responsible.

It's possible to insure your negative, but it's expensive. You may as well take your chances that nothing will happen to your negative.

GENERAL EXPENSES

Telephone $200
Office supplies $100

If you are fortunate enough to borrow equipment (including camera and lenses) from your school and if you have access to your school's editing facilities, the hypothetical budget for your first project feature film will come to about $52,250. Considering a team of ten active partners, each one has to invest roughly $5,300.

TAPE BUDGET

If a budget such as the one given above is out of the question for you, you may consider a taped project. True, you will save a bundle of money, but let us warn you, no commercial distribution company will even look at your film unless it has been shot in 35mm. (Personally, we are puzzled by this attitude. After all, once you see a film on the home-video screen, there is little difference between a 35mm and a taped project.) Fortunately, most film festivals will screen taped projects.

Without a doubt, a taped project is much easier to handle. Though some festivals will accept ½-inch shorts, we suggest that you tape ¾ inch. This holds especially true if you and your active partners produce the first project for the purpose of showcasing your abilities. Our advice is not to rent a Beta camera (it is expensive) but to hire a company to do the shoot. Get a package that includes:

Camera director
Soundman and equipment
Beta camera
Lights

Such a package will cost you about $1,200 daily. Considering a ten-day (weekend) shoot, your package will come to $12,000.

By taping your first project feature film, you will bypass the high invest-ment in raw stock, lab, and sound lab. Since your project will be tape-edited, you won't have to suffer through the time-consuming editing process. You won't have to pay for optical work, negative cutting, and answer prints. And if you are lucky enough that a distribution company is interested in your taped project, you need a 35mm answer print. It will cost about $20,000 to get a ¾-inch Beta taped project transferred to 35mm film.

But again, let us warn you, generally the motion picture industry hasn't yet accepted this method of feature film production.

SAMPLE BUDGET

Camera and sound package (10 days)	$12,000
Editing in camera (including titles) hourly rate	
(including operator)	$35
total for 40 hours	$1,400
Tapes at $14 each	$140
Catering (you will have a smaller crew)	$500

Purchases and rent: Makeup	$200
Props	$400
Petty cash	$100
Total	$16,690
	(or $1,700 for each
	of 10 participants)
Transfer from tape to 35mm	$20,000

Part Two

Producing Your Film

Depends upon the actor's ability to project to an audience	Depends upon the actor's ability to portray emotions in a strongly felt, but natural way
Depends upon the gesture	Depends on subtle movement, such as the tilt of a head, a tiny smile, or even a look that reveals emotions
	The stage actor shows the story to the audience. The motion picture actor is supposed to draw the viewer into the story. Watching a stage play, the audience shares an experience. Watching a film is a one-to-one experience, as the viewer not only participates in the events he or she views but also subconsciously turns into the actor on the screen or the partner the actor addresses.

Stage-trained actors who act in a film tend to overact on the screen, or to go stiff and seem colorless and boring. If you decide upon a stage actor, be fully aware that you'll have to work to get an acceptable on-screen performance from this skilled and talented, but screen-wise inexperienced actor.

Look for actors who have participated in student or nonunion films, or attended classes where they received on-camera experience. These classes are valuable as they not only teach actors basic on-screen acting techniques but also acquaint them with on-screen movements.

As far as the actor's résumé is concerned, don't hold it against him or her if it doesn't show many "credits," but take this as a sign of the applicant's honesty. Be satisfied if the résumé lists:

- On-camera classes (recent date)

- Acting classes (recent date)

- Two or three student films (get the director's name and telephone number so you can check out the reference)

- Two or three stage performances

If the actor brings in a short tape (not more than three minutes) of the scene he or she did on the student films, so much the better (and please, do return the tape promptly).

Don't Rely on the Actor's Head Shot   Head shots, your actor's 8 × 10 glossy photos, can be misleading. Here you have discovered a face you want, a face simply perfect for one particular role. You're ready to cast the actor, but first have the actor read for you. Head shots may exude a vitality that is totally absent from the actor. Head shots can mislead because they don't tell you whether the actor has charisma. The sinister villain might turn out to be a pussycat: the powerful female executive might be a mouse in disguise. The sparkle, the personality, has to be evident the moment the actor enters your office.

Meeting Your Prospective Actors

Many directors, especially first-time directors, like to chat with actors. But unless a reading follows the chat, you are wasting your and the actor's time. Chatting may even prove detrimental to the casting of a given role, if the actor's personality differs widely from the character you expect to see on the screen. Still, a short—very short—chat is valuable as it gives you the opportunity to look for the warning signs that will tell you not to cast this particular actor:

- Nervous
- Overeager
- Chip on his or her shoulder

Don't listen to what the actor says, but note how she expresses herself, and most important, look for vitality.

THE ACTOR READS

Recognize and appreciate the difficulties the interviewee faces. The actor sitting in front of your desk has but a few pages of script at his disposal. He has to deal with scant dialog, has no idea about character relationships, and does not know what incident precedes the audition scene.

Do the auditioning actor the favor of informing him about a character's basic demeanor, attitude, and relationship to other characters. Do this quickly and generally. Do not freeze the auditioning actor into any interpretation. Be ready for a surprise. Quite a few actors will come up with interesting interpretations. Believe it or not, a number of actors will give a first reading that is a camera-ready performance. Be grateful if you find actors of such high caliber. Hold on to them. At least grant them a callback.

But don't be disappointed if most readings fall short of perfection.

One-dimensional Reading   The actor tries to outguess the director and ends up reading the "meaning of the lines," expressing the surface emotions and goals the lines indicate without discovering and dealing with the text's hidden meaning, his subjective reaction to the situation, relationships, and character to be portrayed. Listening to one-dimensional readings, one cannot help but remember the late Lee Strasberg's advice: "Don't ever read so-so right. It is far better to read gloriously wrong."

Hammed-up Reading   Speaking about a "gloriously wrong" reading, we are not speaking about a hammed-up reading. Reading gloriously wrong means the actor brings in a reading that—while wrong for the depicted situation—is filled with true, honestly and naturally expressed emotions. A hammed-up reading, on the other hand, refers either to emotions that are projected too theatrically for the screen, or emotions the actor shows but does not feel. The actor tries very hard to act, but comes across phony.

Laid-back Reading   This kind of overly relaxed reading is preferred by actors (often found in California) who confuse naturalness with unemotional mumbling.

Effective Reading   The moment you discover a reading that shows the following aspects, keep the actor in mind for a callback:

- Natural, but not laid-back, line delivery
- Honest, but not pushed, emotions
- Communication in line delivery
- Reaction to lines read by the casting director
- Thoughts between lines
- And most important: spontaneity

The actor might not exactly conform to the type you had in mind, the actor might even oppose your projected type, but give her the opportunity of a callback. As you cast any major role, opt for the better actor and be less concerned about type. For "under fives" (a role where the actor speaks fewer than five words) the opposite holds true—by all means, go for the type.

As you watch and listen to the auditioning actors, do not expect any of them to read the role as you envision it, but watch for their acting ability.

Once you have decided to call an actor back, you may wish to give more detailed information about the character to be portrayed. Still, always take into consideration the actor's own interpretation. Now is the time to discover the fusion between the fictional character and the actor's personality. For this very reason ask the actor not to work on the script with a coach. You want to evaluate the important personality and character fusion, not the coach's interpretation of the role.

Many callbacks won't bring in the expected results. At times, unfortunately, now that the actor has had the opportunity to work on the script, her reading ends up lifeless and stilted. But don't give up just yet. Try to have the actor remember the honest emotions, the vivid interpretation that impressed you during the first reading. Remind the actor of the character's goal, need, and the physical environment of the scene to be read—in short, try your best directorial skills to get the actor back on track. Suggest two different interpretations. This also would give you some indication of whether the actor is "directable." But don't waste a lot of time trying to get a good reading from any particular actor.

The second callback is the one that will tell you about the actor's screen presence. (If you are working with SAG actors, you'll have to pay for all callbacks, except the first one.) Have the actor perform memorized lines in front of a camera, since it is almost impossible to gauge an actor's on-screen presence with a reading alone. Viewing actors on a monitor might surprise you. An actor whose reading was acceptable but unexceptional may come alive on the screen. Others who gave you a terrific reading may suddenly seem stilted and cold.

CHARACTER TAPESTRY

Select actors who will provide your film with visual diversity. If you have a group of characters—students, for instance—do not cast tall, blond, beautiful girls only, but a cross section of looks and personalities you are apt to find on any campus. If your heroine is torn between two lovers, don't have them both be the same body type and coloring. If you have two attorneys on opposite ends of a trial, do not make them undistinguishable as far as age, looks, and demeanor are concerned.

CHEMISTRY BETWEEN ACTORS

Now is the time to gauge the chemistry between your cast's main characters. How do your lead actors relate to one another? Are they going through the motions or do they really listen to each other and react? Immediately after you have decided upon your cast, go through a general reading of the entire script. Now is the time to replace actors if necessary.

8.

The Director

and the Actor

You've cast actors who are perfect types and you have a great script, so now you can't wait to write the shot list. You want to set camera angles and camera moves and start directing your actors. But hold on—you have some important homework to do before you even begin rehearsals. Even the most perfectly structured script hides all kinds of traps. If you start shooting your movie without a thorough script investigation, be ready for aggravation—and worse, loss of money and time. A good director has to be able to bring in an artistically and technically sound movie, and must bring it in on time and on budget. You can avoid several production problems in advance by investigating your script, not only in view of your film's visual aspects but also in view of performance elements.

There is another reason you ought to begin your directing task with script investigation: once you're on the set (or on location), your attention has to be focused on the use of camera setups and moves to strengthen your actors' performances and to set the scene's mood. This, understandably, leaves you little time to work with your actors on their individual performances or their interpretation of roles. But regardless how skilled and creative your actors are, you are responsible for determining characterization, relationships, and scene buildup.

The purpose of this chapter is to discuss scene structure as it applies to your work with actors. We will be dealing with elements that lead to emotionally effective performances. In this respect we'll have to accept the fact that the motion picture actor, unlike the stage actor, lacks the luxury of the emotional arch. A film actor works on scenes out of sequence and performs in short takes, as opposed to a stage actor, whose ultimate performance will gather momentum from the play's inherent dramatic structure.

The beginning of a scene (a character entering a room, for instance) and the end of the scene, when the character leaves the room, are shot back to back (immediately following each other), while the fragmented core of the scene will be shot later. As such, actors have to deal with the numerous setups of fragmented scenes. Since scenes are not shot in their logical progression, many actors lose their character's emotional arch and fall back on a line reading. (Line reading refers to the detrimental practice of expressing exactly what the written text implies, without delving deeper into the dialog's hidden message.)

The director who wishes to avoid the hidden traps of one-dimensional acting, illogical character development, unrealistic relationships, and monotonous scene flow will do well to investigate the script before and during the rehearsal process. Your main tools of investigation are analysis of facts and assumptions and your attention to the reality of the moment.

Facts and Assumptions

Directing is not so much the literal interpretation of the written text as the discovery of goals and emotions hiding behind the written word. The screenwriter takes great pains to write lines in such a way as to leave plenty of space for the director's creative task of discovering the characters' emotional and physical actions. These actions are based upon given facts and logical assumptions. Facts consist of what a character says about herself and what others say about her. Both lead to assumptions about a particular character, such as what her goals, needs, relationships to others, and conflicts are. When you take a look at each major character and first assess the facts as given in the script, you consequently draw your own conclusions based on these facts and begin to move away from many preconceived (and possibly stereotyped) ideas about the characters, and you get a better idea about molding performances into sensible units.

The following demonstration scenes are taken from the action film *Four Blind Mice.*[*] Considering the brevity and scant dialog of the given scene, these character profiles seem to be sufficient:

> Ahna—a downtrodden homeless woman
> Art—a kind homeless man

Both seem to be one-dimensional characters. So let's get busy and breathe some life into them.

An action script has been chosen to serve as a medium for script investigation because an action film is one of the most difficult projects to tackle. The script depends on action and suspense elements, offering minimal dialog, which leaves little opportunity for characterization. Generally, most action films present stereotypes, skimming over the surface of thorough character delineation. It is the director's job to turn clichéd characters into interesting human beings. Read the following scene and make your own list of facts and assumptions about Ahna and Art.

FOUR BLIND MICE

INTERIOR AHNA'S CAR—DAY

AHNA is curled up in an old car. Clothes and blankets and some household implements are piled in the back of the car. She wears an air force bomber jacket; a field cap covers her eyes. Forcing herself to wake up, she thrashes around. Her fists hit the sides of the car.

AHNA

No . . . no . . . hell no . . .

(Her screams turn into mumbles, as she gradually opens her eyes.)

ART *(voiceover)*

Hi, Ahna . . . wake up . . . look . . .

[*]Adapted from *Four Blind Mice,* a Ciara Production Inc. Film (Renée Harmon, writer-producer), 1992.

AHNA, still groggy, sits up. She pulls her cap back. We see she is an unkempt, disheveled woman.

AHNA's *POV. ART, a homeless man, smiles at her. He holds up a thermos.*

ART
Cafe Nero . . . Cafe Bombay—

He pours some coffee into a plastic container and holds out the cup to AHNA.

ART
Still hot. Got it at the mission.

AHNA rolls down the window. She takes the cup and gratefully sips the hot liquid.

AHNA
Thanks, Art . . . that feels good.

Observing AHNA enjoying the hot coffee, ART leans closer.)

ART
Great grub last night at the mission. Meat loaf, mashed potatoes, corn . . . Why ain't you going with me to the mission?

AHNA
Yes . . . maybe . . . oh, I don't know. But thanks for asking me . . . anyway. . . .

She hands the empty cup back to ART, smiles.

AHNA
You always think of me . . . thank you.

ART
We street people got to stick together, ain't we? How about another shot?

AHNA stretches.

> AHNA
> Why not.

> ART
> How 'bout going with me to the mission?

> AHNA
> Maybe.

> ART
> Come on.

AHNA, obviously afraid to hurt his feelings, gets up and does her chores. Pushing clothing and boxes about, she tries in vain to bring some order to the chaos surrounding her.

> ART
> 'Cause it's a handout? Woman, you've got a lot to
> learn. We've got to survive. We all have to accept . . .
> what ye call it?

> AHNA
> Charity.

> ART
> Yeah . . . charity (he watches her for a beat). How long
> have you been on the streets?

AHNA tries to remember. She folds a blanket.

> AHNA
> They let me go at the hospital.

> ART
> The nuthouse?

> AHNA
> No, not a mental institution, of course not . . . *(thinking hard, every thought a painful attempt)* uhm . . . I guess

that was in May. I went back to my apartment—the
one on—God I can't remember where my apartment
is.

ART, waiting patiently, looks at AHNA with compassion.

> AHNA
> *(a sudden flash of memory)*
> Yes, it's on Crescent—corner Third Street and Cres-
> cent, that big gray building. But then my money ran
> out and they evicted me. I packed up all my things.
> So I must have been on the streets for about . . . three
> months . . . *(now positive)* yes, three months.

> ART
> Woman, you're still a greenhorn, but you'll get with
> it.

Various angles on the homeless.

> ART *(V.O.)*
> I've been on the streets for over a year now. Came all
> the way from Iowa. Figured, hell there's work to be
> had in sunny California. Shit. Figured . . .

BACK ON ART

> ART
> . . . wrong. I'm a construction worker, really good at
> it . . . but they ain't hiring in . . .

ON HOMELESS ACTIVITIES

> ART *(V.O.)*
> . . . this here place. First I stayed in a motel, ate at
> the fast-food places. Then I cut down to one meal a
> day . . .

ON AHNA AND ART

> ART
> ... roomed at a flop house until I ended on the streets.

ART pulls out paper bag. The paper bag contains a small bottle of whiskey. Art uncorks the bottle.

> ART
> This here booze keeps me alive.

FACTS AND ASSUMPTIONS

Ahna

FACTS	ASSUMPTIONS
Ahna lives in a car.	Ahna is homeless.
Her car is stuffed with clothes and household implements.	She owns a car, has some possessions, she belongs to the upper crust among the homeless.
She accepts a cup of coffee from Art, a homeless man.	She accepts friendship.
She declines Art's suggestion to go to the mission for a warm meal.	She feels uneasy in her homeless state.
Again she declines to go to the mission.	Either she is stubborn, or she is emotionally unable to face the reality of her condition.
She cannot remember how long she has been living on the streets.	She may have some mental dementia.
She forgot the location of her former apartment.	Same as above.

She has spent some time in a hospital.	She was lying about being confined to a mental institution or she had some severe or traumatic physical ailment.
She was evicted from her apartment.	She has no means of support.
She is a greenhorn.	She has difficulties adjusting to her situation.

Conclusions, based on assumptions:

• Ahna is a homeless woman who has not yet adjusted to her way of living. She has mobility and some protection from the elements because she still has a car.

• She is sociable enough to be able to accept friendship.

• She has spent some time in a hospital, possibly a mental institution. She has memory lapses or mental confusion.

Director's notes: Do not approach Ahna as the clichéd homeless, gruff, tough street character, but stress her friendliness and her reluctance to accept her present situation. Soft-pedal her obvious memory loss during the initial scenes.

Art

FACTS	ASSUMPTIONS
Art shares some coffee with Ahna.	He takes care of others.
He tries to persuade Ahna to join him at the mission.	He may be a bit domineering.
He advises Ahna to accept her homeless state.	He feels comfortable on the streets.

He has seen better days, but drifted into poverty.

Not much ambition.

He drinks.

Alcoholism?

Conclusions based on assumptions:

• Art is a veteran of life on the streets. He may even consider himself the leader of the group of homeless camping out in a public park.

• He has accepted his way of living, feels rather comfortable, and accepts whatever is offered to him. The mission has become an important part of his life.

• He feels camaraderie with Ahna, and enjoys helping her.

• There is a chance that alcoholism has led him into poverty.

Director's notes: Though the script implies that Art has accepted his way of life, avoid any clichéd interpretation. Depending on the actor's personality, stress either Art's bitterness or his grain of humor.

The Reality of the Moment

In this segment we'll look in detail at scene structure as it applies to actors' performances. Each and every scene, regardless how short or insignificant, constitutes a building block that is significant to your film's entire construction. As you investigate the emotional content of each scene, keep in mind that they must propel the story and your film's relationship patterns and emotional tapestry. Just as you should never lock your actors into your own vision of character interpretation, neither should you hesitate to guide your actors by way of the discoveries you have made during your script investigation. You have to leave your actors plenty of emotional space to roam about, yet keep each individual performance within the framework of rhythm and pace you have created. Not an easy task.

Assume that each actor is more concerned about his or her performance than your film's emotional unity. It is your responsibility to mold your actors' performances into an emotionally cohesive and rhythmic unit. Rhythm refers to a scene's progression, as well as the emotional and/or physical integrity of your actors' individual performances.

It may happen that during shooting and watching dailies, scenes run smoothly. Everything looks great. But weeks or even months later, as you watch your film's rough cut, your joy turns into frustration. The film's rhythm is off—way off. Each scene plays on the same level, or more precisely, all scenes show the same intensity level. You ought to decide upon your film's rhythm—its intensity patterns—long before the first day of photography.

As far as movies are concerned, intensity applies to communication levels and action levels. For communication levels intensity is divided into three degrees:

Intensity I—to explain
Intensity II—to make a point
Intensity III—to force

For example, Ralph and Amy discuss their vacation plans:

Intensity I (to explain)

AMY: Why don't we go back to Santa Barbara? It's such a nice place. We'll go swimming and do some snorkeling, take strolls on the beach.

RALPH: How about Yosemite? I'd like to do some hiking for a change.

Intensity II (to make a point)

AMY: Why Yosemite? It's such a long drive. Santa Barbara is only an hour's drive from Los Angeles. It'll take us eight hours to drive to Yosemite.

RALPH: Be sensible. We went to the seashore last year, and the year before, and the year before that. Why not have a little change?

Intensity III (to force)

AMY: I hate hiking. You wouldn't get me even close to those darned mountains.

RALPH: Really? Don't forget I'm paying for the trip. Yosemite it is.

Be especially aware of communication intensity levels if you are faced with one of the infamous sitting-down scenes. If possible, add movement to these scenes; if not, go for quick successions of two-shots, reversals, and a number of reaction shots. Milk your reaction shots, express a character's true feelings in these shots, express the *unsaid,* and you'll have an interesting film. Make your reaction shots the visual counterpoint to the spoken words. But be subtle; don't have your characters react too predictably, occasionally give the audience the unexpected, and give them a bit of mystery. And most important, vary the scene's intensity levels.

Monotonous intensity will play havoc with your action scenes. Action levels are also divided into three levels of intensity:

Intensity Level I—low
Intensity Level II—medium
Intensity Level III—high

As you shoot your film, the temptation is great to place all emphasis on high-intensity action, and to forget about the human element so important for these segments. Here are some tips on using intensity levels to enhance the rhythm of the action in your film:

· Intensity levels change from scene to scene. If one scene ends at level III, the next scene may continue at level III or it may move to either II or I.

· If one scene ends at level II, and the next one also begins at level II, the second scene must move either up to III or down to I.

· Avoid having a sequence of scenes operate all on level II (also called the deadly two).

· Be sure to build up intensity levels within a scene.

· If faced with exposition, have characters operate on different intensity levels.

While rhythm gives physical and emotional variety to each scene, pace refers to human relationship structures. In this segment, therefore, we'll concern ourselves with scene structure as it applies to the tapestry of relationships between characters. Keep in mind that each scene must propel the story and your film's relationship patterns forward. If a scene fails to do so, omit it or consider a rewrite.

All well-written scenes lend themselves to pacing. Such scenes feature either emotional interest or suspense peaks and valleys. These fluctuations could be strongly stated or subtly indicated. If you, the director, are unable to discern these modulations, then the writer has delivered an unactable scene. Most likely one of these elements is missing:

- The character has nothing to fight for.
- The opposition is diffuse.
- The character's need or goal is weak.
- The scene lacks urgency.

Don't hesitate to ask your screenwriter to:

- Strengthen the opposition
- Add time pressure
- Add an unexpected event
- Create an obstacle
- Increase character's *need*

Need is closely connected to a character's goal or what a character wants to achieve. But a need might refer to a character's obsessive desire to reach a goal or it might point to the character's hidden goal. In everyday situations—and we all have needs—a need refers to the subconscious drive that propels a character to undertake an action such as to achieve a goal and/or obtain an object at a given moment in time. A need is either satisfied or frustrated, and consequently gives rise to another, often stronger need. Your character's needs are either neatly spelled out in the script, or—more interestingly—hidden beneath the lines. Clearly stated needs often lead actors to express whatever the written text indicates without digging any deeper. Exposing needs hidden beneath the dialog produces more believable and exciting acting. In the scene earlier in this chapter between Ahna and Art, there were implicit needs.

AHNA'S NEED: *I want* to hold on to some behavioral fragments of my past, such as pride and self-sufficiency.

ART'S NEED: *I want* to be needed and admired.

Once the scene meets with your expectations, take a good look at the following building blocks of relationships: conflict, need, and shifting dominance.

Aristotle's conflict areas (man against man; man against nature; man against himself) are as applicable today as they were in ancient Greece. When we think about conflict we tend to picture strong emotions, horrendous decisions, and gripping moments of danger and suspense. In actuality, we face conflict every day in mundane ways. Most likely, we're not even aware of being involved in a conflict situation. Here are a few examples:

Man Against Man   You and your significant other are ready to watch TV. You want to watch a newscast and your partner opts for a comedy show. Though neither of you argues, you are faced with a conflict situation. A certain amount of conflict adds spice to life, as well as to your film. It never hurts to have a bit of conflict within your dialog. If you are faced with a boring, but oh so necessary, exposition segment, make it more palatable by having the screenwriter add some good-natured bantering.

Man Against Nature   This deals with the obstacles one encounters, whether mammoth situations or seemingly unimportant incidents. This is the reason that man against nature is the perfect vehicle for either exploiting a comedy situation or giving zing to a tedious scene. A character struggling to close the zipper on a suitcase while dialog moves on and on can add a comic dimension or a physical representation of a character's relationship conflicts.

Man Against Himself   This may deal with life-and-death decisions, or it might refer to an inconsequential matter such as deciding whether to buy an outfit one really doesn't need. Such conflicts are the kind of emotional struggles you need to create believable fictional characters who ignite the audience's empathy.

Consequently, search every scene in your screenplay for conflict areas. Though conflict may not be obvious in the way dialog has been written, have it emerge through your actors' thoughts and actions. For example, an actor can convey to the audience a sense of conflict by the way she handles the props, such as inspecting cups and saucers to make certain each meets her guest's pathologically high standard of cleanliness.

Changes in relationships and/or situations are based upon shifting dominance. In other words, character A, who was dominant at the beginning of a scene, might be subordinate by the end of the scene when character B has found a way to turn the tables. As a director, you can keep the dialog in a scene fluid by shifting dominance. This is also a good technique to remember for camera setups and moves.

A well-paced scene should also have an apex, the point when both partners or adversaries operate from the same level of dominance. Draw attention to it. This is a scene's suspense moment, the dramatic turning point.

9·

The Rehearsal Process

The advice given in this segment deals primarily with rehearsals that take place on the set prior to the camera run-through. Yet the suggestions given are just as valid in case you decide on an extensive rehearsal period before your film goes on the floor. Some motion picture directors, especially those who have a strong stage acting or directing background, shun rehearsals on the set. They prefer to work with their cast weeks before a shoot. Extensive rehearsals:

• Break the ice between director and actors

• Cut down on the amount of time wasted on the set for rehearsals. The director can give her full attention to camera setups and moves

• Give actors the opportunity to experience the arch of emotion, which they won't have when filming short takes on the set

• Allow actors to gain a clearer picture of the director's vision

• Minimize the number of time-consuming adjustments on the set that might be needed if actors' individual interpretations differ.

There are also disadvantages of extensive rehearsals:

· If your directing experience is primarily based on your previous work on stage plays, you may lead your cast into overly "stagy" performances. Though such performances will look great during rehearsals, they will seem stilted on screen.

· If your expertise is primarily cinematic, your demands regarding story, character, and relationships may confuse your actors. It might be better to conduct a few extensive cast readings instead of rehearsals.

Advantages of rehearsals on the set:

· May promote acting that comes across as more natural and spontaneous, since actors have not been pressed into a definite performance

Disadvantages of rehearsals on the set:

· May result in one-dimensional performances because of limited rehearsal time

· May produce relationships and reactions to given situations that are unclear enough to require reshooting, a costly and time-consuming endeavor

Chances are that once on the set the production pace slows down because of "expression" difficulties one or the other actor experiences. These difficulties are not caused by the actor's lack of characterization or poor grasp of situation. The usual culprits are emotional and communication blocks.

Helping Actors Express Emotion

At times an actor is unable to relate to the emotions in the scene or take commands. Some directors ask you to recall something in your life that really frightened you (or made you giddy with happiness, etc.) and experience it again as they shoot. Method acting, also called affective memory, is still popular but we don't recommend it. Events take on different colorations in memory: we remember conditions and feelings differently from the way they were during the actual event. Trying to re-create the emotions caused by an event makes it more difficult for the actor to concentrate on the scene at hand.

Remember, the motion picture actor is forced to go from moment to moment. He concentrates on what is happening now, during the fraction of the scene being shot. Even the most creative and highly skilled actor will experience difficulties as he tries to bring forth honest feelings while going through the same disconnected fragment of an emotion, time after time, take after take. If you ask the actor to apply the emotions created by a past event (affective memory) to the take presently shot, you are asking for trouble. You'll see pushed emotions (emotions the actor acts, not experiences), or a flat unemotional delivery on the screen, as the actor struggles to recall the hazy reactions to past events.

Actors may have to portray situations and emotions they never experienced before. Fortunately, most of us lead fairly normal lives, without the extreme circumstances fictional characters experience. Don't keep on harping on emotions the actor ought to feel but for which he has no frame of reference. As any experienced actor will tell you, goals—either satisfied or frustrated—are what will bring forth honest emotions.

If the satisfaction or frustration of a goal is not sufficient to ignite strong emotions, there are other techniques. Therefore, instead of torturing your actors by lecturing them about the emotions you wish to see on the screen, simplify matters by employing some sense memory (method) exercises. These exercises, all resulting in automatic physical reactions, are based on the five senses.

Instead of concentrating on goal or emotion, the actor focuses on an abstract object to be experienced through the five senses, one that will evoke strong and highly specific emotions. In this respect the actor does not think about the object, but by using her senses, makes a particular object real. The object in turn ignites a specific body condition (positive or negative) and as such leads to experienced (and consequently expressed) emotion. Fortunately, sense memory not only helps you to project never-before-experienced emotions, it also gives you the ability to show honest emotions take after take. It also assists in the expression of those mixed emotions one can hardly put into words.

FIVE SENSE MEMORY EXERCISES

Touch   Situation: the character is happy but hesitant about a new phase in his or her life (getting married, going off to college, etc.). Object: you, the actor, touch an extremely valuable crystal vase. You admire the vase, but you are afraid it may break if you hold on too tightly. Or: Situation: the character has trouble making someone listen to good advice. He or she is extremely frustrated. Object: you, the actor, push a heavy refrigerator.

Sight   Situation: the character is very much afraid of saying or doing something. The character is frozen with fear. Object: you, the actor, watch a tarantula creeping up to you. Object: you, the actor, see a pit bull blocking your way.

Sound   Situation: the character looks forward to an exciting and happy event. Object: you, the actor, listen to your favorite tune.

Smell   Situation: the character has to confront a relative or friend about his or her cheating. Object: you, the actor, smell the odor of garbage or spoiled food.

Taste   Situation: the character rejoices though he or she has achieved a goal in a somewhat devious way. Object: you, the actor, taste the most delicious chocolate candy.

The actor employs objects that are personally meaningful to bring forth the required emotions. If an actor is not frightened by a tarantula, substitute a pit bull. The point is, the actor does not employ sense memory for the actual experience of touching, smelling, hearing, seeing, tasting, but for the emotional response these activities will call forth. Advise the actor to concentrate fully on the emotion-causing object while speaking the lines, and not on the text. And, equally valuable for the expression of honest, truly felt emotions, advise the actor not to control the emotions the sense memory object arouses, but let the sense memory object control his or her actions.

Needless to say, each actor will create his or her own sense memories and not those that affect his or her friends. Before you introduce an actor to sense memory, and to find out whether the actor responds to sense memory, you may wish to conduct this little exercise:

• Decide upon an object. It is important that this object does *not* evoke any emotion. Something you use every day, perhaps your toothbrush.

• Close your eyes and picture the object (toothbrush) suspended in front of you. Try to *see* colors, shape, and so on.

• Keeping your eyes closed, raise your hand and *explore* the object with your fingertips.

• Ask yourself: Did the object become real at any given time?

Some fine and skilled actors are not sensitive enough to respond well to sense memory. If so, don't waste any time on sense memory but use the positive and negative reaction technique.

In life there are only two basic emotions: we like something (positive) or we dislike something (negative). It's as simple as that. While you experience a positive emotion, your body is relaxed and you smile. If you experience a negative emotion (fear, anger, sorrow, uneasiness), your body is tense. Take a good look at people in your environment: you can tell by their body language how they feel at the moment.

Unfortunately, often actors are not aware of this correlation between body language and vocal expression. If the actor is tense for personal reasons—maybe she is unsure of her lines—her body is tense while she speaks happy (positive) lines. On the opposite side of the coin, the laid-back actor may mouth angry (negative) lines while slouching about. Both types of performances are unsatisfactory for the simple reason that the actor's body stands in contrast to verbal expression.

Should you decide to employ the acting tool of positive and negative reaction, do not translate this technique immediately to the actor's lines. Photograph the actor as she goes through these little exercises:

POSITIVE REACTION

Have the actor relax her body, then smile. Positive reaction comes in three general degrees:

NEGATIVE REACTION

Have the actor tense his or her shoulders. (Do not permit any frowns or facial distortions.) Negative reaction (regardless of the emotion to be expressed) comes in three general degrees:

Positive I: a small smile (you like something a bit)

Negative I: tense shoulders

Positive II: a medium smile (you rather like something)

Negative II: tense shoulders and tense stomach muscles

Positive III: a great big smile (you are euphoric about something)

Negative III: tense shoulders, tense stomach muscles, and clenched fists

Make the actor aware that the physical response to positive and negative emotions correlates with one's physical reaction to real-life situations.

The next step is to have the actor do the following in positive or negative reaction mode: count to ten, recite a nursery rhyme, point out items in his or her environment ("this is a table," "this is a chair," "this is my script.") Once the actor feels comfortable with the correlation of physical state and verbal expression, begin rehearsing lines. Though the positive and negative reaction technique does not bring forth expressions as emotionally charged as sense memory does, it will result in an honest on-screen performance.

Helping Actors with Characterization

Many actors and directors see characters in a static, stereotyped way. They stress:

- Occupation, social background, educational background
- Age
- Lineaments (posture, facial expression)
- Speech

In other words, if one casts a doctor, the doctor will have a different look from an Amish farmer. The housewife will move differently from an heiress. This type of characterization is sufficient for simple, one-dimensional characters, but as you work with your costarring and starring actors, you ought to take a more complex view of characterization.

PRIMARY SENSE OF BEING

Physical characteristics, occupation, social background, educational background, age, and lineament are only part of a character's primary sense of being. It also includes the combination of mental and emotional attitudes that force a character to act and react in very specific ways.

Always be aware of the fusion of character and actor as you discuss characterization, and take the actor's personality into account. It is the combination of the actor's personality (charisma) and the character's personality that make for exciting on-screen performances. But be careful to avoid two traps:

• Don't permit the actor's charisma to overshadow or eliminate the character.

• Do not stress character to such an extent that the actor's personality gets lost in the process. If you do, an interesting and alive character will end up hollow on screen.

Using the assumptions you have gained from your script investigation, you have arrived at a character's composite personality, one that depicts a character's mental, physical, and emotional state, as well as the way the character operates under most conditions. The character's relationships to other characters and his or her reactions to a given situation are based upon these mental attitudes. Remember the old admonition "Never have your character act out of character," and take into consideration:

- Background
- Frame of reference
- Mental attitude: intelligence, opinions about life and people
- Emotional attitude: desires, moods, display of affection or dislike, aggressiveness, submissiveness
- Lineament
- Health
- Environment
- Main trait—positive or negative
- Complementary trait—positive
- Complementary trait—negative

- Weak point, that causes trouble
- Strong point, that saves character
- Point of recognition, the moment when a character's strong point (or weak point) overpowers the opposite point

If you have an overpoweringly strong star, or a weak one-dimensional star, surround him with interesting characters. Do not rely on your star's charisma, but concern yourself with your film's overall tapestry.

SECONDARY SENSE OF BEING

Often the character's primary sense of being and the actor's primary sense of being blend easily. Still, the actor may be far enough removed from a scene's emotional, environmental, and occupational aspects to encounter difficulties. That's the time when the director will explore a character's state of mind, physical condition, and most important, the motive that makes a character react to a very specific moment in time (the take on hand), by paying close attention to:

- Time
- Place
- Climate
- Character's physical condition
- Character's emotional condition
- Relationship to other characters
- Obstacles
- The character's personal rhythm; is he or she a thinker (introvert) or doer (extrovert)
- Where a character has been prior to the scene to be shot, where he or she will be going (or will be doing) after the scene has been completed

Handling Dialog Problems

Some dialog reads well but sounds a bit on the stilted side once the actors deliver it. Some dialog doesn't read as great but sounds terrific once you watch your actors on the screen. The director's job is to help the actors read believable lines, and that means you must have an ear for the way people speak. Age, socioeconomic status, and relationships between characters are just a few of your guideposts. Give your actors the opportunity to make the lines (without changing one word) their own. Remind your actors that:

• People speak mostly in short sentences (easy to do—just chop long sentences into comfortable bite-size pieces).

• People take time to think, so why not add a thought before a line, in the middle of a line, or after a line?

• Don't speak from comma to comma, or period to period, but adjust lines to your own speech rhythm.

By adhering to these suggestions you will be surprised how much more lifelike dialog sounds. As you intercut verbal expression with thought, be aware that thoughts have to be either in reference or in contradiction to actions and lines. The combination of thoughts and spoken words may either hide or reveal conflict, emotions, or goals.

All through your script you will find hot and cool narration. In no way does this force you to have your actors deliver the dialog in the emotional content as written. Be stronger than the word; be creative; make words come to life—without changing one line.

Hot Narration Hot narration delves deeply into a character's soul, thoughts, and feelings. Hot dialog is truly emotionally charged. If used in moderation such dialog grips your audience. Yet, if used indiscriminately, hot narration may make your film top-heavy with emotions.

Cool Narration Cool narration neither hides nor reveals anything. What you hear is what you get, and mostly you'll get information. Information, though necessary, is boring. Therefore, you may wish to have your characters and/or your camera move about during extended cool-narrative dialog scenes.

Emphasis should be divided between the two types of dialog. As the film moves to its climax, as each scene gains momentum and urgency, dialog will grow hotter. But even then, a short interlude of cool narration will give the audience a welcome respite.

No matter whether hot or cool, your film's dialog ought to be alive with human emotions, goals, and needs. Ask yourself:

- Does dialog, as written, reveal goals and needs?

- Does dialog offer conflict?

- Is information given clearly and simply?

- Does dialog reveal relationships?

- Does dialog reveal emotions?

- Are motive and reaction realistic?

If the script lacks any of the above, have a writer's conference and discuss changes. Don't leave it to your actors and your editor to resolve problems that would be better remedied by a minor script modification.

All About Scheduling

Regardless of whether you intend to produce a feature film or a five-minute short, scheduling—fondly called the filmmaker's paper war—plays an important part in your project's success or failure. We are presenting a feature film schedule, but you should follow the same basic outline when planning shorter projects.

Preproduction Schedule

Once financing (partnerships, grants, loans) is in place and no major script changes are anticipated, your preproduction schedule goes into full force. First of all, do not rush your project. Take your time and realize you'll have a long climb ahead of you. About three months should be sufficient to mount your production.

MONTH 1

- Itemize and finalize your budget
- Look at locations

- Do location breakdown
- Send out casting notices
- Director begin script investigation
- Send out notices regarding the crew
- Get quotes from equipment rental firms
- If film (35mm, 16mm, or Super 8):
    Get price of raw stock (short ends)
    Get quotes from labs (developing, printing, timing)
    Get quotes from sound labs (sound transfer, MAG, Sound FX, foley, mix)
- Get quotes from optical lab (if applicable)

MONTH 2

- Begin casting sessions
- Interview prospective crew members
- Fine-tune the script
- Finalize equipment rental
- Have art director collect props
- Finalize all lab and equipment rentals
- Finalize locations
- Finalize your cast
- Finalize your crew members
- Set light plots
- Shoot lighting and makeup tests
- Check out camera and sound equipment
- Buy raw stock
- Rehearse cast (if applicable)

MONTH 3

- Shoot
- Assemble your publicity material (press kit)
- Do postproduction

This schedule is based on the assumption that students cannot work full-time on their short. If done properly preproduction, production, and postproduction for a film (not video) short might take between two and four months.

Production Schedules

The day before a shoot, the producer's responsibilities are to:

- Confirm locations

- Write daily call sheet (see sample)

- Arrange with director of photography to pick up equipment

- Have AD (assistant director) call actors regarding call times

- Have production assistant call crew regarding call times

- Have art director pick up props and wardrobe

- Go over the next day's shot list with the director and the director of photography. Since it is the producer's responsibility to keep the shoot moving, now is the time to decide whether the shot list needs adjusting:
  Whether any setup might be consolidated or omitted.
  Whether establishing shots ought to be done only on an expensive exterior location and lengthy dialog be shot later, on an insert stage.

Every day the producer has to write the producer's report:

- Numbers of scenes shot (based on location breakdown)
- Exposed footage
- Incidental expenses (petty cash)
- List of checks written

Postproduction Schedule

Again, do not rush things. A six-month postproduction period for a feature film will give you enough breathing space to do things right.

MONTHS 1 through 5

- All phases of editing, including sound editing
- Opticals
- Get your press kit ready
- Mail publicity to film festivals

MONTH 6

- Negative cut
- Answer print
- Final print
- Publicity mail-out
- Have film transferred to three-quarters- and one-half-inch tapes

SAMPLE LOCATION SCRIPT BREAKDOWN

TITLE: *Four Blind Mice* Sequence 2, Page 1

INTERIOR AHNA'S CAR

LOCATION: Lawndale Park DAY: XX NIGHT:

ADDRESS: 1805 Cirrus Street, Lawndale

CONTACT: Al Smith, 764-3288

TOTAL SCRIPT PAGES:

SCENE NUMBER (1) & SYNOPSIS
Ahna wakes up, Art offers her some coffee. Dialog re mission and handouts.

SOUND
  Sync

BITS AND ATMOSPHERE
  none

CAST AND WARDROBE

Ahna
  Long skirt
  Top
  Coat
  Sweater
  Shawl
  Boots
  Cap

PROPS
  Thermos
  Mug
  Blankets
  Pillows
  Purse
  Pots and pans
  A few books
  Old calendar
  Boxes

Art
  Jeans
  Skirt
  Jacket
  Cowboy boots

SOUND EFFECTS
  none

SPECIAL EQUIPMENT AND CONSTRUCTION
  Ahna's car

LIVESTOCK
  none

SAMPLE SHOT LIST

7:00   Crew call
7:00   Makeup call

9:00   Exterior Ahna's car: 2   *(on Ahna and Art*
                                   3   *on Ahna*
                                   4   *Reversal on Art*
                                   5   *Reversal on Ahna*

	6	*Pan with Ahna*
	7	*On Ahna and Art)*
12:00	102	*(On Ted approaching*
	115	*On Ted leaving*
	103	*Ted and Ahna*
	107	*Ted and Ahna*
	110	*Ted and Ahna*
	112	*Reversal Ted*
	113	*Reversal Ahna*
	114	*Walking Two Shot Ted, Ahna*
	115	*Pull in on Ahna)*
2:00–3:00 Lunch Break		
3:00–3:30 Interior Ahna's car	1	*(On Ahna and Art)*
4:00 Exterior Park		*(fight between homeless men and Art)*
	341	*(Art falls back—shot*
	343	*Clem runs in*
	344	*Clem hovers over Art*
	345	*Ratso grabs Clem)*
4:30	346	*Various angles and fight Clem, Ratso (full shots, medium, reversals, and CU)*
	340	*Art runs to car*
	342	*Art rises (special makeup) (apply makeup during Clem, Ratso fight)*
6:00 Wrap		

(The above shooting schedule covers about five minutes' actual on-screen time.)

SAMPLE CALL SHEET

LOCATION:		CALL TIME:	
ADDRESS:		PHONE:	
DATE:			

CATEGORY	NAME AND PHONE#	TIME IN	TIME OUT
Producer			
Director			
Assistant director (AD)			
Production manager (if applicable)			
Production assistant (1) (PA)			
Production assistant (2) (PA)			
Script supervisor			
Camera director			
AC			
Focus			
Soundperson			
Boom person			
Gaffer			
Best boy			
Electrician			
Slate			
Key grip			
Assistant grip (1)			
Assistant grip (2)			
Makeup			
Assistant Makeup			
Art director			
Assistant to art director			

TALENT	NAME	PHONE #	AGENT'S NAME AND PHONE #
Call		First shot	Lunch
Second shot		Wrap	
Exposed footage			

Part Three

Launching Your Film

claim involving copyright, contents, and credits of respective films or videos submitted."

It is not uncommon for a film festival to reserve the right to copy your submission for publicity or educational broadcast.

Generally committees judge your entry for:

- General interest
- Production value
- Educational value
- Aesthetic value
- Creativity
- Overall impression

While you are prohibited from submitting any material that has been exploited commercially, you are free to submit any film you have submitted to other film festivals, regardless of whether your film has been awarded a prize. Label the package with:

- Your name
- Film's title
- Running time
- Return address

Distribution

Once your first project feature film has gained favorable recognition at film festivals, either a distributor may get in touch with you, or you may wish to contact one. Forget about megafirms like Universal, Warner, or Disney. Concentrate your efforts on distributors of intelligent art films, such as Sony-Classics.

If a distribution company accepts your film, it will run through three distribution stages. A few release prints will be printed only for domestic theatrical distribution to play during the off-season in a few multiple-screen theaters. Next, the distributor will lease the film to a home-video distributor, and to cable and TV. Third, your film will be released to the foreign film markets.

Don't expect to make a fortune on your film. Most distributors consider that they are granting you, the beginning filmmaker, a favor by handling your film. If you make a few dollars, if you see your and your partners' investment returned, you are among the fortunate few. Look upon your first project's distribution as but another one of the unavoidable dues you'll have to pay on your way to becoming a professional filmmaker. But even if a company offers to distribute your film, don't be led down the road of blissful ignorance.

Find out about the particular distribution company that is interested in your film. Check out state superior court records to discover any claims against said company. And if things look just a bit too good, watch out. *Have an entertainment lawyer go over your distribution contract's fine print.* Most distribution contracts are boilerplate, preprinted contracts that go on and on. Your attorney will point out any ambiguous clauses and demands. After all, distribution contracts favor the distributor, not the producer.

We cannot examine an entire distribution contract, but here are the most pertinent items.

Distribution period   Most distributors ask for perpetuity. It is more beneficial to the producer to stipulate a time limit, say, three years.

Rights granted   The distribution company will demand all rights to your picture, including the copyright. Only a filmmaker with a track record will be able to keep important rights (music, home-video, merchandising) for himself. Make certain that all rights, and especially the following, are spelled out:

   • The right to distribute the film for the following media, domestic and foreign: theatrical, home-video, cable, and TV

   • Music, publishing, and merchandising rights

   • The rights to all underlying rights (have all these rights listed)

Delivery   You will supply your film and other requested materials. For example, with foreign distribution only, you must deliver a copy of your script for translation and dubbing.

• Film: original negative, optical sound track negative, three-track master of the sound track, answer print, color-corrected interpositive, titles, background used for title, M&E track, outtakes and trims, and television cover shots, if applicable

• Trailer: picture negative, optical sound track negative, textless background, sound track

• Publicity: stills (black-and-white, color) color slides

Unless you are producing a film for a major studio (Universal, Disney), it is better if you cut (to the distributor's specifications) a trailer and deliver it yourself. You have to pay for the trailer anyway, and distribution-company-cut trailers cost much more than those made by the filmmaker. In any case, your distributor must have the film, trailer, and publicity shots to fill overseas orders. However, if you deliver all of those items you lose control over your film. See if you can deliver a release print and keep your negative in the lab's vault. As the distribution company requires a number of release prints, have them agree to have your lab print them. Try to negotiate this before signing the contract. You might not get it, but you can try.

In case you have signed additionally for home-video, cable, and TV distribution, deliver the following items:

• Video: digital video master, one in NTS format and one in PAL format (overseas buyers demand PAL)

• Cable: digital television master, one in NTS format, one in PAL format

For foreign sales you may deliver all of the above items or grant your distributor *limited* access to the lab where your property is stored. (We'd opt for the latter.) Unlimited access is acceptable only if the distribution company has financed part of your film.

Editing "The distributor reserves the right to reedit the picture." Either have this clause omitted altogether or have it clearly spell out which segments are supposed to be reedited and what the extent of the reediting will be.

Documents

• Original screenplay, synopsis of screenplay, script supervisor's notes (don't discard any during production), music cue sheet, dialog spotting list, credit list, talent contracts

• If your screenplay has been copyrighted, submit a copy of the copyright certificate

• Music licenses (if applicable)

• Notarized assignments of rights (if applicable)

Warranties

• Producer warrants to keep distributor free of liens and claims

Make certain that these claims do not pertain to any claims connected to the distribution of your film, but to the film per se, such as unpaid debts, invasion of privacy, or libel claims.

• Producer warrants that all third-party participation has been disclosed.

• Producer warrants that he or she has the right to enter into agreement.

Security Interest "Producer will grant distributor security in the film (. . . title)." Do not agree to this clause unless the distributor has substantially invested in your picture. Be aware that distribution expenses, such as publicity and release prints, do *not* fall within the realm of contributions—money put up by the distributor for the actual shooting of the film.

Distribution Expense (collection and tranversion, licenses, and export fees) Make certain that part of expenses, such as travel to foreign film markets, booth rental, and entertainment expenses are not added to your account.

Advertising Expenses Try to set a limit on advertising expenses. And keep in mind that for domestic theatrical exhibition, distributors and exhibitors share the expenses of newspaper and TV advertising. Make certain you receive a list of expected expenses, and insist that any further advertising expenses require your written consent.

Distribution Fees   Distribution companies charge the following:

• A 10 percent (or higher) interest rate on what they spend on release prints and advertising

• A 30 percent domestic distribution fee from monies collected (domestic theatrical)

• A 35 percent distribution fee for all markets (theatrical, home-video, TV, cable) overseas. If your distributor works with foreign subdistributors another 10 percent will be tacked on

• A 20 percent fee for domestic auxiliary markets (home-video, cable TV)

• A 5 percent gross participation fee, based upon the entire amount of gross receipts received domestically and foreign

The gross participation fee is unjust. But since you have to pay it, make certain that all fees are listed separately.

Advances to Producer   For your first project, there won't be any.

Claims   "Producer shall hold distributor and its subsidiaries, officers, and representatives harmless from obligations arising from claim damages." This clause positively requires clarification. Have your attorney take the position that this clause is unnecessary as it has been covered by the warranty clause. If the distributor, however, should insist upon it, have your attorney add, "Distributor grants identical warranties to producer."

Errors and Omissions Insurance   Depending on your film's theme and subject, you might consider purchasing such insurance.

Producer Is Responsible for Residuals   This clause comes in effect if you have cast SAG actors. It pertains to TV and cable sales only.

Gross Receipts—Domestic   We have arrived at the most complex point in our discussion. First, gross profit derived from domestic theatrical exhibition is based upon box office or the exhibitor's (theater owner's) income from ticket sales. From this amount, the exhibitor deducts the floor, which means expenses pertaining to rent, upkeep, overhead, and salaries. Next, the exhibitor deducts her share of the advertising expenses (remember, these expenses are carried fifty-fifty by both exhibitor and distributor). The remaining profit will be split fifty-fifty with the distributor.

Then the distributor deducts these expenses:

- Taxes
- Overhead
- Shipping charges
- Release prints (eventually the producer will have to pay for these in addition to the aforementioned 10 percent interest rate)
- Advertising expenses

It is to your advantage to have your attorney change gross receipt to adjusted gross receipt. Gross receipt refers to the entire amount of money the exhibitor (theater owner) took in. Adjusted gross receipt refers to the actual amount delivered to the distribution company. From the gross the exhibitor deducts his expenses, such as movie theater rental and upkeep, administrative expenses, salaries, and his part of advertising costs. Since the producer (filmmaker) has to pay distribution expenses to the distributor, and since these expenses are based on percentages of gross or adjusted gross, the producer is better off to have his percentage taken off the lower adjusted gross. It is not an easy process, and it takes a tough attorney to get an adjusted gross deal.

Gross Receipts—Overseas   Overseas distributors will lease your film from your distributor for a flat sum. This sum may be as small as $2,000 (for all rights—theatrical, home-video, TV) or it may be more than ten times that. For your film, a small independent production, do not expect to receive more than $2,000 to $5,000 per territory.

Yet, considering that your film may sell in a number of territories and may sell for more than one year, you could make a tidy profit. The foreign distributor deposits a letter of credit (LC) in your distributor's account. The letter must be deposited before your distributor will deliver all the items pertaining to foreign distribution. After your distributor has deducted her expenses and distribution fee, you'll collect the monies due to you.

Home-Video Receipts   If your distributor handles all the rights, you are pretty well at the distributor's mercy. Most likely the company handles your film *because* of its home-video prospects. However, chances are that a film that is of no interest to a distributor may find its niche through a company that handles home video exclusively. Here is some advice in reference to such a scenario:

• By all means insist upon an advance if you deal with a home-video distributor. An advance might be all you'll ever see.

• Have the home-video distributor agree on a release date. If not, your film may languish on the company's shelves for months.

• Once the distribution company has recouped the advance paid to you, it will pay royalties based upon your tape's wholesale price, less distribution cost.

• You won't receive payment on all the tapes shipped out; a number of tapes will be returned. And don't forget that feature film tapes have a rather short shelf life.

Cable and TV   There is no way you can possibly handle cable and TV sales yourself. Most likely your distributor will include your film in a package that accommodates TV's late-night movie slot. About twice a year you will receive some royalties.

Net Receipts   Here we are speaking about the insidious practice of granting the producer 100 percent of the net profit. As we advised previously, net profit does not exist. It's 100 percent of zilch.

SELF-DISTRIBUTION

Over and over one hears beginning filmmakers talk about "four-walling," the practice of renting a theater, printing out flyers, and paying for ads in local papers. This practice of putting your film on the screen is not viable any longer. It was a questionable way of showing your film even in the long-gone days of the mom-and-pop movie houses. Now, since theaters are owned by big chains, don't even dream about four-walling.

12.

Your Future in

Film and

Video Production

The assumption of this book is that you are seriously interested in one day having either a job or a career in some aspect of film production or the electronic media. There is a lot of competition. No matter what position you have your eye on, there are many, many other folks out there who want it just as much as you do, maybe more. This can be very discouraging at times, but it should not put you off your goal. People get in every day, so anything is possible. Stay focused, work hard, learn your craft, develop your network, and trust that sooner or later all this will pay off for you.

The following list does not pretend to be exhaustive, but it should give you some idea of jobs and careers that are available in film production and in the electronic media. The arrangement does not imply any prioritization; it is simply a convenient way of organizing the material.

First, you should know that in order to work in the industry on a regular basis, many positions still require some kind of union affiliation. Today, however, there is a great deal of nonunion film production that provides opportunities to do the same jobs, and, in fact, most entry-level jobs will probably be in nonunion productions. Today, as the economy changes and the once powerful craft unions lose much of their influence, many professional filmmakers regularly move back and forth between union and nonunion jobs in order to keep working.

Above-the-Line Jobs

PRODUCING

Producer is one of the most ambiguous job titles in the industry. There are all kinds of producers, and many of them are producers in name only. They have the title because they raised some money, worked out a deal, or happened to know somebody. In feature films, a writer who has sold an original screenplay may negotiate a producer credit on the film, but this rarely means that the writer has any real power in the actual decision-making process. It is not unusual for a writer with the producer title to still not be welcome on the set.

Having said that, producing is a legitimate and important position in both film and television. Producers essentially put together all the elements necessary for the film or television program to work. Among other things, they hustle to put projects together, they make the deals, they do the hiring and firing, they struggle to keep huge egos and volatile personalities in line, and they push everyone to keep moving so they can bring the project in on schedule and under budget. Often they are in the position of saying no, and this brings them into conflict with writers, directors, actors, and others. Because of the difficult nature of their jobs, they are often disliked. When a project is successfully completed, usually everyone involved takes credit and receives public acclaim—everyone except the producer.

Sound like your kind of job?

Actually, there are people who thrive on this work and do it very well. If you are well organized and can pay attention to details, if you have a lot of determination to finish what you start, if you can effectively exercise authority and get along with all kinds of people (some of them not very nice), if you have lots of chutzpah and a very thick skin, then maybe this is just the career for you.

Independent Producer   An independent producer is basically someone who puts projects together and tries to get them made. She may be temporarily affiliated with a studio or production company, but essentially she works freelance. Most do lots of hustling and many of them have long periods of little or no income. If they are between projects, they are no longer on payroll, and, unless they have an established production company with substantial assets, this can create severe personal and professional hardships. They never want to speculate with their own money, but sometimes this is impossible not to do. Much of independent producing is a kind of crapshoot—you are betting that all the long hours and hard work will eventually pay off. Unfortunately, there is no guarantee that it ever will. It is not unusual for an independent producer to make several hundred thousand dollars one year and be on unemployment the next.

Line Producer   The man or woman who is "in the trenches" throughout the preproduction, production, and postproduction is the line producer. He is on the set or on the location, trying to keep everything moving and trying to solve whatever problems come up during shooting. He struggles to do a careful balancing act, trying to support the above- and below-the-line talent so he can make the best-quality film or video he can, while at the same time trying to adhere to the budget and scheduling restrictions. Sometimes this puts him in an impossible position as he tries to please both the business and creative interests at the same time. It is often a thankless task, but most productions absolutely must have an individual doing this important work or the film will never get off the ground.

Writer-Producer   This producer has an extremely important position in television. In fact, one may generalize and say that if the theatrical motion picture is the director's medium, network television is the producer's. Television producers (working with the network or cable companies) control the shape of the show, whereas the various episodic directors are essentially hired hands. If you look at the credits on series shows, especially situation comedies, you will often see several producers listed. Most of these are probably writers, or at least they began as writers. They started as a freelancer, then as part of a staff, then eventually managed to negotiate a producer credit. These hyphenates (as they are called) have become very powerful and influential in today's industry.

DIRECTING

How do you become a director? If you are a student in a radio-TV-film program, your production group may agree for you to take on the job. Or you and some friends may scrape up enough money to do a low-budget horror film, and you are tabbed to direct. Possibly you know a rock band that wants you to do a music video for them. Perhaps you've written a particularly good script and a producer is willing to give you the opportunity to direct it. Or at some time you may achieve success in another area, such as acting, and you might use that success to move into directing. The point is, there are many ways to become a film director.

What does it take to be a successful director?

A lot. A good director has to have an aesthetic sensibility, a certain amount of technical competence, and an ability to collaborate with others in a way that inspires trust and confidence. She must have a strong visual sense, an understanding of basic dramatic structure, and the capability to understand and communicate with actors. On top of all that, the director should be a determined and focused individual who has boundless energy, common sense, good judgment, clear insight into human psychology, and, perhaps most important, is absolutely in love with her work. Of course, the director has a number of very specific responsibilities to carry out. Some of these have already been discussed in greater detail.

Directors who work regularly in the industry usually join the Directors Guild of America since most studios, networks, and major producers are signatories to the minimum basic agreement between the guild and the producers. The guild not only covers film and television directors but also a number of other positions.

Unit Production Managers   This job is similar to that of a producer, though unit production managers usually spend a lot of time working out of an office and making hundreds of phone calls every day during production. One of their major responsibilities is to create and maintain an accurate shooting schedule that will allow the film to come in on budget. The unit production manager is the coordinator of all the technical aspects of the production and needs to have good managerial and organizational skills to keep things running smoothly.

First Assistant Director   This person is essentially the director's right-hand man (or woman). The first AD is on the set or on the location and usually stationed at the director's side during filming. He is in charge of the crew and basically runs the set, freeing the director to concentrate on the creative side of the filmmaking process. The "first" may also direct extras and stage certain actions under the supervision of the director, and may at times coordinate the shooting of second-unit material. First assistant director is a production-oriented job and is *not,* as some people suppose, the next step to becoming a director. In fact, very few working directors moved into that position from working as an AD.

Associate Director   This is a title used in videotape production. This job has responsibilities that are quite different from those of the first AD in film. On a multicamera shoot (like a taped situation comedy) the associate director works in the booth with the director, rather than on the set. The AD often moves the cameras into position and presets the shots so the director can focus on calling the show. In many cases, the AD also supervises the editing of the episode as well. Interestingly, the AD in video production *does* sometimes move up to directing (which is logical, if you think about the job description).

Second Assistant Director   The second assistant director works under the first and is responsible for a lot of the paperwork that has to be completed during production. She keeps the time sheets, distributes the call times, moves actors to and from the set, and generally does whatever the first assistant needs her to do. She is often the first one on the set in the morning, the last one to leave at night, and the one who gets yelled at the loudest when things go wrong. It is possible to move from second to first, and indeed many do so after putting in the prescribed number of hours.

Today the best way into the system is through the trainee program sponsored by the Directors Guild of America. This annual competition provides an opportunity for a select group of applicants to work as trainees on feature films and on television series for a two-year period. They are paid a bit more than $350 a week for their work and once they accumulate 400 hours on the job, they are qualified to join the DGA as a second assistant director. The competition is fierce: out of several thousand applicants, only eight or ten are selected each year. The hours are long and the work is hard. However, the program does open the door to membership in the guild and to a career as an assistant director. If you are interested in pursuing this avenue, you should contact Elizabeth Stanley, the administrator of the DGA trainee program at the Directors Guild of America in Los Angeles.

WRITING

Here is another industry truism: *if you want to be a writer, you have to write!* And keep writing. And keep writing. Even when you can't get your stuff read. Even when you are rejected over and over again. Even if you never sell anything or never get an assignment. You just have to keep on writing.

Establishing a career in professional scriptwriting is difficult. It is hard to break in, and it is even harder to stay there. Currently there are approximately 10,000 members of the Writers Guild of America, and a relatively small proportion of them are actually deriving all their income from writing. A few years ago an analysis of writers' credits indicated that fewer than 300 writers were producing almost 90 percent of *all* television programming. That's rather startling, if you think about it.

However, in spite of the competitive nature of the field, in some ways writing is the easiest way to break into the industry. It's one of the few things you can do that is not dependent upon someone else. It costs you only the time you spend at the word processor or the typewriter turning out your masterpiece. Of course, as anyone who's tried to do this realizes, it is not as easy as all that, but if you have the talent and creative energy, script-writing might be your entrée.

It is true: people in the industry really are looking for good scripts. If you are persistent, you can find someone to read your material, and if you picked the right person, it could very well be the big break you have dreamed about. As in everything else, however, you must take the time to learn your craft. How do you do this? Enroll in scriptwriting classes. Watch movies and television programs. Read as many scripts as you can get your hands on. Study dramatic structure, characterization, and dialog. And by all means, *learn the proper screenplay format and proofread your work!* Incorrect grammar, misspelled words, sloppy syntax, and pages filled with typos do not make favorable impressions! You won't get that many opportunities to have your script read, so you want to make sure it is as good as you can possibly make it before you send it out.

One way of learning about writing is to work as a reader for an agency or a production company. Readers go through the massive amount of material submitted to agents and producers and make a preliminary judgment about its potential. Typically, they write a summary and a short critique, and then indicate whether they recommend the script and/or the writer for consideration. These short three- to four-page summations are then passed on to the production executive, who may then make a determination about reading the complete script.

Because so many scripts are circulated in this industry (and many of them are just awful), readers provide a necessary service for busy executives. They have no real power themselves, but they do act as gatekeepers and can certainly be instrumental in moving a script along to a decision maker. There are a number of professional readers, of course, but you might be surprised to learn that many readers are college students, secretaries, production assistants, beginning writers, or friends of the producer. Most young people who do this work find it extremely educational because they get an opportunity to read scripts written by their competition, and they can then compare both the good and the bad to their own work.

ACTING

The inevitable rejection actors experience can become very personal. A performer places himself on the line. It is his face, body, and voice that are being judged and found wanting, and sometimes this takes an emotional toll on the person. It has been said that most actors have a bit of the exhibitionist in them. After all, they are putting themselves on display all the time. But, at the same time, actors also suffer from a sense of insecurity that is only exacerbated when they are told over and over again that they "aren't quite what we're looking for." Even actors who are working regularly—even major stars—have this sense of insecurity because they know they may not last long.

If you know that and still want to be an actor, then you need to prepare yourself. It is true that there are certain intangibles about successful performers that cannot be taught. Some have it, others don't (whatever "it" is). We recognize screen presence when we see it, but we are hard-pressed to explain it. Even so, there is much about acting that can be learned. It, too, is a craft that involves mastering certain disciplines. Good actors are constantly growing and perfecting their performance techniques throughout their entire careers. They know there is *always* something more to learn.

Preparing yourself to act professionally involves training—a lot of training. You might major in theater in school or college. Certainly you will want to audition constantly and try to land as many roles as you can. Working on the stage is still one of the best foundations for actors. Many professionals who make their living in television or in commercials still do live theater, often for little or no pay, in order to do what they consider to be "real acting."

In order to work in film or television, or if you hope to do commercials, you should enroll in acting workshops that will provide opportunities for you to work *on camera*. It is crucial that you see yourself on tape so you can understand the specific demands of the medium and can make the necessary adjustments in your mannerisms and delivery. There are many such workshops, and most of them advertise in trade publications like *Drama-Logue*.

Another way to get on camera is to appear in student and independent films. College and university film and television programs are constantly looking for nonunion actors who will work without pay. It is great experience, and usually you can negotiate your own videotape copy of the production in exchange for your appearance. Sooner or later you will need to put together a demo reel that shows what you can do, and working in such productions may give you a few good scenes for that purpose. Naturally, as you move on and land a commercial or a guest appearance on a television show, you should make copies of this work for your reel.

You will need good photographs of yourself—specifically, 8 × 10 glossy head shots that show you exactly as you are. There is nothing more exasperating to a casting director or an agent than to call someone in based on their head shot and discover that they look nothing like their picture! Since this photo will be your calling card and may well be the difference in whether anyone calls you for an interview, you better get it right. It is worth the investment to have them done by a professional photographer so that you come off at your very best.

You should try to determine what type you are. This may be distasteful to you, but the fact is that much casting is based on type initially, especially in television and in commercials. If you are a wholesome ingenue type, for example, then those are the parts you'll be reading for. No one is going to ask you to play Maggie in *Cat on a Hot Tin Roof*. If you are a "character type" (and that could mean most anything), chances are you will never be seriously considered for a leading role. This is another reason that a number of television actors do stage work. It permits them to act "against type" and to take on roles they would never have an opportunity to play otherwise.

Professional actors are members of the Screen Actors Guild, or SAG (which governs work in film), and/or the American Federation of Radio and Television Artists, or AFTRA (which governs work in audio and video). You cannot join SAG until you actually have a job with a signatory company, but you may join AFTRA by paying the current initiation fee. After you work one time for a signatory company, you *must* join the appropriate union if you hope to continue working in the industry.

The Screen Extras Guild governs professional extras, but there are a lot of nonunion extras working in the industry today, especially on location. Some young actors mistakenly believe that they can become an actor by working as an extra first, that a director will spot them among the crowd and give them their big break. Unfortunately, it rarely works that way. The role of the extra is *not* to stand out, but to blend in. Extras who do this for a living want to be able to work as many shows as possible, even appearing in different roles in the same film, and to do that they have to be something of a chameleon. Many of them have wardrobes for all occasions, wigs, even disguises that permit them to change their look.

Acting in film or television appears glamorous, and it is. It is also very hard work that is often frustrating and emotionally draining. In addition to talent, determination, and a willingness to learn and to grow, it also requires a very special kind of belief in yourself that will see you through some very hard times.

Below-the-Line Jobs

There are many craft and technical positions in filmmaking and video production. We will list only a few of them here, focusing on some of the major categories, just to give you an idea of what may be available.

CAMERA

The principal position related to the camera is the director of photography. This is the person responsible for the look of the film. In consultation with the director, she will select the film stock, the lenses, the camera, lighting style, the color scheme, and anything else that bears on how the image will appear on screen. Most DPs do not operate their own camera. They are hired for their "eye," based on what they have done in the past. Some directors have favorite DPs with whom they work from one film to the next because they are confident that this person will be able to capture on film or video precisely what they want. Director of photography is a union category (either IATSE or NABET), and is a very difficult position to achieve.

Other camera positions include the operator, who actually runs the camera, the focus puller, the loader, and the camera dolly grip. All are union positions in major productions, either film or television. Of course, in nonunion filmmaking these positions may be combined. On a low-budget feature, it is not at all unusual for the DP to operate his or her own camera and to work with only one camera assistant. This is not permitted in union situations, however. That is one reason that on a union set you will see four persons "working camera," and that does not include the director of photography.

Breaking in as a camera operator with the hopes of moving up to DP means that you must shoot a lot of film and video in order to put together a representative demo reel of your work. Today it is very helpful if you can work in both media, especially if you find yourself trying to make a living as a freelancer. One DP who has spent more than twenty years shooting low-budget features on 16mm and 35mm film now finds himself almost exclusively shooting commercials and industrial videos on Betacam.

SOUND

The sound mixer is responsible for recording all the live audio in a production. Again, working in consultation with the director, he or she will decide how best to mike the scene. Part of this determination will include whether the producer wants production-quality sound or whether the live audio is essentially a scratch track to be replaced later by automated dialog replacement (ADR). The sound mixer works with a Nagra sync recorder or a mixing console that is usually located somewhere off the set. In television production, the sound mixer is usually situated in the audio booth.

Boom Operator　Working with the sound mixer is usually at least one boom operator who is responsible for placing and manipulating the microphones on the set.

Other key jobs in sound are found in postproduction. In most major films, the sound track is built or put together in the mixing stage. There will be many tracks of dialog, effects, and music that must be combined into a single sound track.

Foley Artist Besides the ADR already mentioned, there will be "sweetening" and "foley" work. A foley artist supplies sounds, like footsteps, door knocks, and numerous other effects that must be synchronized with the film's action.

In order to work sound on a major feature film or on a network television series, you must be a member of either IATSE or NABET. However, there is a lot of nonunion production going on today that provides opportunities for people interested in this aspect of production. One may start by doing the sound on student films, or by working on a low-budget feature as a cable puller or boom operator. It is possible to gain experience both from working on nonunion films and videos and from apprenticing yourself to a sound technician who may be willing to show you how the job is done.

LIGHTS

The key person involved with lighting a set or location is the gaffer. He or she will have a best boy and several lighting assistants. The gaffer works under the direction of the director of photography and it is his or her job to execute the plan for the look of the film or video. A gaffer must have a genuine aesthetic sensibility in order to create the style and mood the director and the DP want. He or she must be able to work with colors, create and eliminate shadows, control direction and intensity of light sources, and know the effect of color temperature on film and video. Gaffers must also understand the properties of electricity, such as wattage of instruments and current capacity of power sources. On top of all this, gaffers must be able to do their work quickly and efficiently. Much of the waiting around on a set is often due to the time involved in lighting the scene. Since time is money in filmmaking, gaffers who can keep things moving while still achieving the appropriate look are worth their weight in gold.

Gaffer is a union position, but again today many gaffers work both union and nonunion shoots. Like other key technical jobs, you learn about lighting by actually doing it, either working on student and other nonunion films and videos, or by landing a position as an assistant to a gaffer on a major shoot. You should be aware that lighting demands on student and nonunion productions may not be at the level demanded in the industry, so you want to be careful about picking up some bad work habits.

Other Positions on the Set

There are a number of other job categories that are prominent on a film or video set. Script supervisors stay near the director and are responsible for maintaining the continuity of the show. Grips are in charge of moving everything from the camera to sections of scenery. Set designers and art directors are responsible for the physical look of the set, including the period style, and the selection of colors and textures. There are people who "dress" the set, and others who supply the props. There is often a makeup designer and a costume designer, who will each have a number of assistants.

Action shows will require stunt coordinators, some of whom are also directors, and they will work with a team of stuntmen and -women. Some shows use special effects supervisors, and they are often called upon to supply gunshots, fires, explosions, and even hurricanes. There may be a greens man, who takes care of supplying trees and plants, a schoolteacher, who conducts classes for any children who may be working the shoot, and a state welfare worker, whose job it is to look out for the health and safety of the children. There will be several members of the Teamsters Union, who are responsible for driving all the vehicles, including the portable dressing rooms and the "honey wagons" (rest rooms).

In some instances there will be police officers and firefighters on the set. There will be caterers who supply everything from round-the-clock snacks to full-course meals. In addition, there will be all manner of producers, assistants, and gofers who provide support for the artists and technicians. Sometimes when visiting the set of a major motion picture you will see 80 to 100 people milling around the location, and it is hard to imagine what they all do. Yet most of them actually do have specific responsibilities related to the filming, and most of them are likely members of a union.

Postproduction

A major part of postproduction is editing, putting together the images and sounds that make up a film or video. Often the process begins while shooting is still going on, when assistant editors sync dailies or log video footage, and the editor begins to make a rough assembly of shots. This gives the producer and director an idea of what they have "in the can" and might suggest some adjustments or additional shots than can be undertaken before the cast and crew are dispersed.

The editor's main work begins once principal photography or the primary video production has been completed. Guided by the script supervisor's detailed notes, and working closely with the director—and in video production, working closely with the producer(s)—the editor cuts the visuals and sounds into some kind of narrative continuity that has the appropriate pace and rhythm. He will work with the raw footage until it is edited together in the most dynamic way possible, hopefully to the extent that it is not only dramatically effective but also layered with a certain amount of subtext, metaphor, and even symbolism.

Good editors are vital to the success of any production. Their importance is underscored by the comment that is heard quite often during many shoots: "We'll fix it in post!" Though an editor is obviously limited by the quality of the original materials he or she has to work with, it is nevertheless true that many a film or video has literally been "saved" by some timely and creative editing. Much of the success of Steven Spielberg's *Jaws* was due to the input of Universal editor Vera Fields, and the dramatic structure of Stanley Kramer's Academy Award–winning film, *High Noon*, was more or less created in the editing room.

In major film productions, the editor will have a number of assistants who do the necessary syncing and logging chores. Once the show is cut to the satisfaction of the director and the producer, then other artists take over. Often in feature films and in some television shows, much of the original sound is stripped and an entirely new sound track is created from scratch. Major portions of the dialog may be replaced by ADR, especially if it was shot on a noisy location, and almost all the background sounds may be taken out and re-created in the studio. Working closely with the appropriate sound technician, the music editor pulls together all the music, whether it be from a licensed music library or from a specially composed score. The effects editor cuts in all the sound effects and background ambient sounds. It is not unusual for a final mix of a major motion picture film to involve twenty or thirty separate sound tracks, maybe more.

Good editors are in demand today, especially those who edit video and are familiar with nonlinear editing systems. A number of films and video programs are already being edited on computer-based systems, such as those produced by Avid, and more shows are coming online. The advantages are many. Once all the footage is stored in the system, either on video or on laser disks, the editor has instant access to every scene by either clicking on a mouse or punching in a few keys on a computer keyboard. It is much easier to try alternative versions of scenes and to make changes using such a nonlinear system than it is using analog tape systems or traditional film-editing systems, whether Moviolas or flat beds. If you think you might be interested in a career in editing, you would do well to find an internship or an apprenticeship that will provide you with an opportunity to learn as much as you can about nonlinear editing and digital postproduction.

A Few Notes on the New Technologies

We can only imagine what future technology will be like and how it will affect the entertainment industry, but we do know that it will be connected to computer and digital technology. We are already seeing the pervasive presence and use of the computer in every aspect of production—in preplanning, scriptwriting, breakdowns, budgeting, scheduling, editing, mixing, and special effects—and this use will only increase. In some areas, the impact of the computer is nothing short of revolutionary. It has such power to manipulate the pixels of images stored in its memory that it has led one special effects expert to declare that "the truth of photographic reality is dead." There is not a film or video image that cannot be manipulated digitally (just look at what was accomplished in *Forrest Gump*). What will this do to the work of the cinematographer, when everything he or she puts on film, including quality of color, light, and exposure, can be altered after the fact in the computer?

What about the digital rights to a performance? Suppose you act in a film and receive payment for that work, but your image, voice, and mannerisms are digitized and stored in a computer's memory bank somewhere. You—or at least an electronic representation of you—could then appear in other films, in commercials, and in video games without you ever stepping in front of a camera again. Technically, this is possible right now—expensive, not very practical, but possible. Should you be paid in perpetuity every time your electronic self appears? This raises some interesting issues that are quite understandably receiving a great deal of attention from the Screen Actors Guild and AFTRA.

The increased use of interactivity will continue to have a significant impact on the direction production takes in the future. We have already seen a number of experiments in this regard. The short theatrical film *Mr. Payback* gave audience members the option to instantaneously select alternate versions of scenes by manipulating an electronic switch, and there are some very complex interactive video games on the market now. Some of these have been produced on budgets that rival those of independent feature films and star recognizable actors, like Mark Hammel. Incidentally, a script for these interactive entertainment programs may very easily run several hundred pages in order to include all the possible story options.

There will most likely be a lot of jobs opening up for you in film production and in the electronic media that don't even exist right now. That is one of the exciting things about starting out as you approach the transition from one millennium to another. And remember this: no matter what direction technology takes us, the film and video industries will still need people to supply the content, to develop the software, so to speak. It will need energetic, forward-thinking men and women with imagination, creativity, and a willingness to work hard—all qualities that you can develop right now.

Appendix A

SUPREME COURT OBSCENITY RULING

The current standards were established in 1973 (*Miller* v. *California,* 413 US 15), and courts currently attempt to determine "whether the average person, applying contemporary community standards, would find that the work, taken as a whole, appeals to the prurient interest; whether the work depicts or describes in a patently offensive way, sexual conduct specifically defined by the applicable state law; and whether the work taken as a whole, lacks a serious literary, artistic, political, or scientific value."

This attempt to define obscenity is rather vague, and the Supreme Court has yet to rule directly on whether indecency and obscenity are synonymous. But the Court has given considerable leeway to local prosecutors in their interpretation of "community standards," so that what might be actionable in the Midwest Bible Belt may not be in San Francisco's North Beach. However, there are certain subjects, most notably bestiality and the whole area that deals with the sexual exploitation of children, that will be prosecuted anywhere at any time.

Since the production and distribution of obscene material are against the law, it is clearly *not* the direction you want to go if you hope for a career in legitimate film or electronic media production.

• • • • • • • •

Appendix B

FADE IN:

EXT. WATERFRONT—VARIOUS ANGLES—DAY

Summer. The rustic waterfront of a small town on the east coast of Florida. Small sailboats; charter fishing boats; at the far dock, a few shrimp boats. SEAGULLS swoop down past the weathered pilings, soaring and dipping, their mouths open wide as if they are squawking to one another—but we do not hear their calls.

BROWN PELICANS fold their wings and dive in tandem, their heavy bodies crashing into the choppy water—but we do not hear the splash.

*Adapted from *Heart of Silence* (Jim Lawrence, writer), 1996.

In the shallows, a WHITE HERON with greenish-yellow legs pokes around among the sea grasses and flushes out a school of minnows; and further out beyond the channel markers, a FRIGATEBIRD flies low across the rippling surface, its long cleft tail flowing majestically behind—*all in silent pantomime.*

In fact, we do not hear the distant roar of the ocean, the lapping of the waves, or the rush of the wind. We hear only the sound of SOFT BREATHING and a RHYTHMIC HEARTBEAT.

EXT. PIER—DAY

16-year-old LISA DEAN leans against the railing and stares in utter fascination at the gulls and pelicans that dance and dart around her. She is a slight, willowy girl with auburn hair and large, sensitive eyes. She wears an oversized F.S.U. sweatshirt, faded jeans, and frayed tennis shoes with no socks.

We MOVE IN CLOSE on her face as she follows the flight of the birds, hungrily watching every free, unbound movement.

As before, there is no sound—except for the BEATING OF HER HEART and the WHISPER OF HER BREATHING.

CLOSE ANGLES—BIRDS

We see the mouths of the gulls, calling incessantly; we see the pelicans, splashing in the water and gulping up fish—still in pantomime.

CLOSE ANGLE—LISA

She stares—anxiously, eagerly, straining to . . . HEAR! *If only she could* HEAR!

Suddenly, a rough hand grips her shoulder and spins her around, startling her.

EXT. PIER—DAY

A coarse, muscular WORKMAN pushes by her, balancing one end of a heavy creosote-covered timber on his shoulder.

Immediately, ALL THE LIVE SOUNDS OF THE WATERFRONT ARE NOW PRESENT. We are almost overwhelmed by the SUDDEN DIN.

> FIRST WORKMAN
> (sharply)
> Want your damn head knocked off? I told you to get
> th' hell out of the way!

He moves past, followed by a SECOND WORKMAN, who carries the other end of the heavy beam.

> SECOND WORKMAN
> What's th' matter with you, girl? You deaf or some-
> thin'?

Lisa is flustered, embarrassed. She quickly moves aside and backs away down the dock.

CLOSE ANGLE—SEAGULL

It soars toward the CAMERA, mouth open—and this time we hear the abrasive SQUAWK.

EXT. HIGH ANGLE—WATERFRONT—DAY

Lisa hurries down the wooden dock and moves rapidly along the waterfront, as the SOUNDS of the once-silent environment crescendo.

FOLLOW SHOTS—LISA AT THE WATERFRONT (VARIOUS)

Lisa moves along the water's edge, passing the shrimp boats, the marine supply yards, the stacks of posts and timbers, the bait stands.

FOLLOW SHOTS—LISA IN TOWN (VARIOUS)

Lisa turns and soon she is moving through the business district of the sleepy, riverside community, passing local FISHERMEN, BOATERS, and occasional TOURISTS. We ESTABLISH the picturesque, semi-tropical setting. We continue to ESTABLISH Lisa's deafness, in contrast to the proliferation of SOUNDS around her.

EXT. POST OFFICE—DAY

Eventually Lisa arrives at the main post office and hurries inside expectantly.

INT. POST OFFICE—DAY

She quickly moves to one of the small boxes and looks inside.

ANGLE—MAIL BOX

There are several pieces of mail visible behind the glass.

INT. POST OFFICE—DAY

Lisa eagerly works the combination and takes out the mail: a circular, some "occupant" material, the utility and phone bills—and a personal letter postmarked "MIAMI" with the scrawled return address of "A. J. DEAN."

Lisa can scarcely contain her excitement as she opens the envelope and quickly moves toward the door.

EXT. POST OFFICE—DAY

Lisa happily moves out of the building, totally engrossed in her letter.

FOLLOW SHOTS—LISA IN TOWN (VARIOUS)

Lisa passes various colorful local landmarks while reading her letter. Along the way there are INCIDENTS that occur because she is more interested in what she's reading than in what's going on around her.

She almost steps in front of a MOTORIST who is making a right turn. He angrily leans on his horn and SHOUTS at her.

A KID whips by on Rollerblades and startles her.

EXT. SEAFOOD RESTAURANT AND BAR—DAY

Eventually Lisa approaches a small seafood restaurant and bar—certainly not one of the five-star establishments. She returns the letter to its envelope, peers in through the front window, then enters.

INT. SEAFOOD RESTAURANT—DAY

This place is a "joint." It's one of those neighborhood places with pretty good food, reasonable prices, and very little pretense. The "atmosphere" consists of a large swordfish mounted on the wall and some draped mullet nets containing seashells and starfish.

There are quite a few PATRONS inside—in fact, it's pretty crowded and noisy. A jukebox plays COUNTRY AND WESTERN MUSIC.

Lisa makes her way to the counter and takes a seat on one of the few empty stools. She looks around expectantly until she finally sees the person she is looking for.

Lisa's mother, 36-year-old MAGGIE DEAN, is busily moving about from table to table, trying to wait on the many customers. She is an attractive woman who is a little "shopworn" in appearance. She tries to retain a youthful posture in a uniform that is tight on her ample figure. At this moment she is frazzled and harassed as she tries to cope with the noontime rush.

At one point she sees Lisa. She moves over behind the counter, retrieves the hamburger and french fries on it, and places it in front of Lisa.

Maggie speaks rapidly and tersely, with little regard for Lisa's handicap. This makes it very difficult for the girl to follow her meaning.

> MAGGIE
> You're late again. The stuff's prob'ly cold by now.

Lisa starts eating her hamburger. Her mother disappears to respond to a PATRON'S request. The following conversation takes place with an increasingly harassed Maggie darting back and forth from the counter to the various booths and tables.

> MAGGIE
> (continuing)
> You won't be able to eat free no more. Mr. Muncey told me today we gotta pay from now on . . . so you'll have to fix yourself somethin' at home.

Lisa tries to follow, but with her mother bobbing in and out as she talks, she finds it rather difficult.

> MAGGIE
> (continuing)
> You wash out that underwear, like I told you?

Lisa nods "yes."

> MAGGIE
> (continuing)
> You get all th' ironin' done?

Lisa shakes her head "no."

> MAGGIE
> (continuing)
> Well, you do it before I get home. I got a date with Ed
> tonight and I want to wear that red dress. I left it
> right out where you can find it, so don't do the wrong
> one, like you did last time.

Lisa looks uncomfortable at the mention of the man's name. Suddenly, she
remembers the mail and digs the various letters and bills out of her pocket.

> MAGGIE
> (continuing)
> That all we got?

She shuffles through it quickly.

> MAGGIE
> (continuing)
> Nothin' but bills an' advertisements.

Hesitantly, Lisa takes the letter out of her pocket and shows it to her mother.

> MAGGIE
> (continuing)
> What's that? Another letter from A.J.? I thought I
> told you to quit writin' him.

She whisks away with an order. Lisa frowns and gently returns the letter to
her pocket before her mother comes back.

MAGGIE
(continuing)
What'd you do with it?

Lisa starts to reach for the letter, but Maggie stops her.

MAGGIE
(continuing)
Never mind. He ain't got nothin' to say I want to hear. (beat) I don't know why you keep on writin' him when I tell you not to. (shouting to a customer) I'm comin'! Keep your pants on!

She hurries off, leaving Lisa alone with her cold hamburger and french fries. She stares at her reflection in the mirror. Somehow she's managed to lose her appetite.

EXT. ROOMING HOUSE—DAY

The late-afternoon sun shines on a rather run-down, weather-beaten "beach type" rooming house. The peeling paint, the rusty screen door, the warped boards on the outside chairs, and the ill-kept yard suggest that the building has definitely seen better days.

INT. DEAN APARTMENT—DAY

CAMERA MOVES about the small, cramped, and cluttered apartment. It consists of a combination living room/kitchen, an adjacent bedroom (with no door in between), and a closet-size bathroom.

Among other things, the front room contains a sleeping cot and a small black-and-white television set, which is turned on VERY LOUD to an afternoon soap opera.

Lisa stands by the portable ironing board, running an iron over some wrinkled clothes (mostly her mother's). She only half pays attention to what she is doing, as she glances out the torn screen and through the open window.

She is lost in her own world and pays no attention to the program BLARING FORTH from the TV set.

At one point there is a KNOCK on the door behind Lisa. It grows louder and more insistent.

> MRS. PARRISH
> (O.S.) (calling loudly)
> Hello! Anybody home? Hello!

INT. HALLWAY—DAY

MRS. PARRISH, the landlady, a dumpy, frowzy woman in her fifties with an ash-laden cigarette dancing out of her large mouth, pounds on the door.

> MRS. PARRISH
> Will you turn that thing down in there! (muttering)
> Gettin' so it sounds like a crazy house around here.

Exasperated at the lack of response, she tries the door, finds it unlocked, opens it, and steps inside.

INT. APARTMENT—DAY

Mrs. Parrish registers disgust at the state of the apartment, and annoyance at the fact that Lisa seems oblivious both to her presence and to the NOISE.

With a SNORT, Mrs. Parrish marches over and shuts off the set. Her sudden presence startles Lisa. The big woman edges closer, looking around with obvious displeasure. When she speaks, she addresses Lisa in a mixture of muttered asides and loud, overly exaggerated pronouncements that might be directed toward a severely retarded child.

> MRS. PARRISH
> Now look here, honey. I know you don't hear too
> good, but you just got to keep that TV set turned
> down. YOU ... UNDERSTAND ... ME?

Lisa nods, apologetically, trying to read the lips clamped down on the cigarette.

MRS. PARRISH
(continuing)
They's other tenants in this buildin' besides you an'
your mama, an' I been gettin' complaints. I say, I . . .
BEEN . . . GETTIN' . . . COMPLAINTS!

She continues her inspection, moving about the room, glancing into the bedroom with raised eyebrows.

MRS. PARRISH
(continuing)
This is a nice place. I won't have no riffraff givin' it a
bad name. No I won't. You understand? I say . . . I . . .
WON'T . . . HAVE . . . NO . . . RIFFRAFF . . . HERE!
(beat) You tell that to your mama when she gets
home. I say, TELL . . . THAT . . . TO . . . YOUR . . .
MAMA!

Again, Lisa nods. She's inwardly praying for the woman to leave her alone.
Finally, Mrs. Parrish moves to the door, muttering.

MRS. PARRISH
(continuing)
Just wastin' my breath . . . can't hear a word I say . . .
just looks at me . . . like a damn moron . . . law, sometimes I don't know what I do to deserve this . . .

She moves out of the room and down the hall. Lisa looks after her, then casts
her eyes back out the window. We HOLD on her face and—

DISSOLVE TO:

EXT. RIVER INLET—SUNSET

A lone shrimp boat is silhouetted against the setting sun as it returns from
a day on the ocean. It is followed by a flock of hungry seagulls.

• • • • • • •
Appendix C

FILM FESTIVALS

California

AFI Los Angeles International Film Festival
Los Angeles Independent Film Festival
Marin County Italian Film Festival
Orange Coast College Film/Video Department Festival
Riverside Film Festival
San Diego Film Festival
San Francisco International Film Festival
Film Arts Festival, San Francisco
Short Attention Span Film & Video Festival, San Francisco
San Francisco International Asian-American Film Festival
Cinequest Film Festival, San Jose
Santa Clarita International Film Festival
Wine County Film Festival, Sonoma

Colorado

Aspen Film Festival
Telluride Film Festival

District of Columbia

Film Festival D.C.

Florida

Florida Film Festival, Miami

Illinois

Chicago International Film Fest

Massachusetts

Boston Film Festival
Brookline-Science Fiction Movie Marathon

Michigan

Ann Arbor Film Festival

Minnesota

Rivertown International Film Festival

New York

Hudson Valley Film Festival
The Big Show Festival, New York City
The New York Film Festival, New York City
New York Underground Film Festival, New York City

Oregon

Portland International Film Festival

Pennsylvania

Philadelphia Festival of World Cinema

South Carolina

World-Fest Charleston

Texas

Austin Film Festival
SXSW Film Festival

Utah

Sundance Film Festival

Virginia

Virginia Festival of American Films, Charlottesville

Washington

The Seattle International Film Festival
Seattle Asian-American Film Festival

For addresses of respective film festivals, please contact the local chamber of commerce.

• • • • • • • •

Appendix D

FOUNDATION CENTER
(FREE-FUNDING INFORMATION CENTERS)

The Foundation Center is an independent national service organization established by foundations to provide an authoritative source of information on foundation and corporate giving. The Foundation Center provides publications and supplements useful to grant seekers:

- The Foundation Directory 1 and 2
- The Foundation 1000
- Foundation Fundamentals: A Guide for Grant Seekers
- Foundation Giving
- The Foundation Grant Index
- Foundation Grants Quarterly
- Foundation Grants to Individuals
- The Foundation Center's Guide to Proposal Writing
- Literature of the Nonprofit Sector

- National Directory of Corporate Giving
- National Guide to Funding (User Friendly Guide) Series

Reference Collections

The Foundation Center
79 Fifth Avenue, 8th Floor
New York, NY 10003
(212) 620 4230

The Foundation Center
312 Sutter Street, Room 312
San Francisco, CA 94108
(415) 397-0902

The Foundation Center
1001 Connecticut Avenue, NW
Washington, DC 20036
(202) 331-1400

The Foundation Center
Kent H. Smith Library
1422 Euclid, Suite 1356
Cleveland, OH 44115
(216) 861-1933

The Foundation Center
Suite 150, Grand Lobby
Hurt Building, 50 Hurt Plaza
Atlanta, GA 30303
(404) 880-0094

Many public libraries throughout the nation carry the above-listed publications. For information in reference to the library closest to you, please call
800-424-9836.

• • • • • • • •
Appendix E

RESOURCES

Organizations

Academy of Motion Picture Arts and Sciences
8949 Wilshire Boulevard
Beverly Hills, CA 90211

Academy of Television Arts and Sciences
5220 Lankershim Boulevard
North Hollywood, CA 91601

American Federation of Radio and Television Artists
(AFTRA)
6922 Hollywood Boulevard, Eighth Floor
Hollywood, CA 90028

Directors Guild of America
7920 Sunset Boulevard
Los Angeles, CA 90046

110 W. 57th Street
New York, NY 10019

Screen Actors Guild
5757 Wilshire Boulevard
Los Angeles, CA 90036

Writers Guild of America
7000 W. Third Street
Los Angeles, CA 90048

555 West 57th Street
New York, NY 10019

Newspapers and Periodicals

American Cinematographer
P. O. Box 2230
Hollywood, CA 90078-2230

Back Stage
1515 Broadway, 14th Floor
New York, NY 10036-8901

The DGA Magazine
7920 Sunset Boulevard
Los Angeles, CA 90046

5700 Boulevard #120
Los Angeles, CA 90036-3659

Drama-Logue
1456 N. Gordon
Hollywood, CA 90028-8409

The Hollywood Reporter
5055 Wilshire Boulevard, 6th Floor
Los Angeles, CA 90036-4396

The Journal of the Writers Guild of America, West
8955 Beverly Boulevard
West Hollywood, CA 90048

Videomaker
P.O. Box 4591
Chico, CA 95927

Books

Aristotle. *Poetics,* with an introductory essay by Francis Fergusson. New York: Hill and Wang, 1961.

Armer, Alan. *Directing Television and Film.* 2nd ed. Belmont, California: Wadsworth, 1990.

———. *Writing the Screenplay: TV and Film.* 2nd ed. California: Wadsworth, 1993.

Bare, Richard L. *The Film Director.* New York: Macmillan, 1971.

Barr, Tony. *Acting for the Camera.* New York: Harper and Row, 1982.

Bradbury, Ray. *Zen in the Art of Writing.* New York: Bantam, 1990.

Dancyger, Ken. *The Technique of Film and Video Editing.* Boston: Focal Press, 1993.

———. and Jeff Rush. *Alternative Scriptwriting.* Boston: Focal Press, 1991.

DiMaggio, Madeline. *How to Write for Television.* New York: Prentice Hall, 1990.

Dmytryk, Edward. *On Screen Acting.* Boston: Focal Press, 1984.

———. *On Screen Directing.* Boston: Focal Press, 1984.

Egri, Lagos. *The Art of Dramatic Writing.* New York: Simon and Schuster, 1960.

Field, Syd. *Selling a Screenplay: The Screenwriter's Guide to Hollywood.* New York: Dell, 1989.

Fridell, Squire. *Acting in Television Commercials for Fun and Profit.* New York: Harmony, 1986.

Gelbart, Larry, Cy Coleman, and David Zippel. *City of Angels.* New York: Applause, 1990.

Goldman, William. *Adventures in the Screen Trade.* New York: Warner Books, 1983.

Gradus, Ben. *Directing: The Television Commercial.* New York: Hastings House, 1981.

Harmon, Renée. *The Beginning Filmmaker's Guide to Directing.* New York: Walker, 1993.

Hindman, James, Larry Kirkman, and Elizabeth Monk. *TV Acting: A Manual for Camera Performance.* New York: Hastings, 1982.

Hunter, Lew. *Lew Hunter's Screenwriting 434.* New York: Putnam, 1993.

King, Viki. *How to Write a Movie in 21 Days: The Inner Movie Method.* New York: Harper and Row, 1988.

Kosberg, Robert. *How to Sell Your Idea to Hollywood.* New York: Harper, 1991.

Mamer, Bruce. *Film Production Technique: Creating the Accomplished Image.* Belmont, California: Wadsworth, 1996.

Mayeux, Peter. *Writing for the Electronic Media.* 2nd ed. Madison, Wisconsin: Brown and Benchmark, 1994.

Morley, John. *Scriptwriting for High-Impact Videos.* Belmont, California: Wadsworth, 1992.

Musburger, Robert B. *Single-Camera Video Production.* Boston: Focal Press, 1993.

Pincus, Edward, and Steven Aschen. *The Filmmaker's Handbook.* New York: Penguin, 1984.

Reichman, Rick. *Formatting Your Screenplay.* Lexington, Kentucky: Book-Smiths, Inc., 1994.

Richards, Ron. *A Director's Method for Film and Television.* Boston: Focal Press, 1992.

Sams Publishing. *On the Cutting Edge of Technology.* Carmel, Indiana: Sams, 1993.

Seger, Linda. *The Art of Adaptation: Turning Fact and Fiction into Film.* New York: Henry Holt, 1992.

———. *Creating Unforgettable Characters.* New York: Henry Holt, 1990.

———. *Making a Good Script Great.* 2nd ed. Hollywood, California: Samuel French, 1994.

Stuart, Linda. *Getting Your Script through the Hollywood Maze.* Los Angeles: Acrobat, 1993.

Vogler, Christopher. *The Writer's Journey: Mythic Structure for Storytellers and Screenwriters.* Studio City, California: Michael Wiese Productions, 1992.

• • • • • • • •
Appendix F

Example of a $1 million budget.

GENERAL BUDGET OUTLINE*

Above the Line

Storyright	$30,000
Producer's unit	70,000
Direction (including agents fee, pension, and welfare)	25,000
Cast (including agents fees, pension, and welfare)	170,000

Below the Line

Prod staff	37,000
Extra talent	7,000
Set design	14,000
Set operations	25,000

*Reneé Harmon, *The Beginning Filmmaker's Business Guide (Financial, Legal Marketing, and Distribution Basics of Making Movies)*, Walker and Company, New York, 1994.

Set construction	70,000
Special effects	40,000
Set dressing	15,000
Property	30,000
Wardrobe	5,000
Makeup and hairstyling	10,000
Electrical	30,000
Camera (including raw stock)	40,000
Production sound	11,000
Transportation	5,000
Location expenses	50,000
Lab	31,000
Second unit	5,000
Stock shots	2,000

Postproduction

Film editing	25,000
Music	5,000
Postproduction sound	12,000
Postproduction film and lab	30,000
Optical FX	5,000
Titles	7,000

Other Charges

Insurances	17,000
General expenses	8,000
Fees, charges	5,000
Legal fees (1.2% of budget)	12,000
Finder's fee (5% of budget)	50,000
Contingency*	153,000

*The amount designated for unexpected expenses and/or underbudgeted items.

Index